UPHOLSTERY RESTORATION

David James

Guild of Master Craftsman Publications

1861 080 522   1202

First published 1997 by
Guild of Master Craftsman Publications Ltd
166 High Street, Lewes
East Sussex BN7 1XU

© David James 1997

Photographs by David James

Drawings by David James

Cover photograph by Ray Highnam
(chair supplied by Tristan Williams)

ISBN 1 86108 052 2

Designed by Teresa Dearlove

Set in Sabon

Printed and bound in Singapore under the supervision of MRM Graphics, Winslow, Bucks, UK

Colour separation by Global Colour (Malaysia)

645.4

UPHOLSTERY
RESTORATION

To Jessica and Amelia

Acknowledgements

My sincere thanks are due to: Angela Burgin;
David Collins; Rod Dean; Graham Giles;
Richard Green; Norman Griffiths; Len Rentmore;
John Rutland; John Turner; Tristan Williams;
and Eddie and Jean Wilson who have all
generously given of their time and allowed me
to use their interesting pieces of furniture
for restoration of the upholstery.
My special thanks are due to: my wife Eirlys;
my editor Jonathan Ingoldby;
and Elizabeth Inman of GMC publications
for her constant support and encouragement.
I would also like to thank the Faculty of Design
at Buckinghamshire College, High Wycombe.

Contents

It is said that the following entry
was made by Thomas Chippendale
in his diary, late one evening
in December 1749:
'Today I went down to see the
upholsterers, but now, having
taken refreshment and rested,
I am feeling so much better.'

Introduction

Traditional upholstery has undergone something of a renaissance during the last twenty years. Whereas prior to this time to 'reupholster' a period piece generally meant tearing off all the original upholstery, burning it as useless, and reupholstering as the individual upholsterer saw fit, there is now a welcome resurgence of interest in sensitive and informed restoration of pieces, sympathetic to their period characteristics.

Nowadays it is reassuring to see the present generation of upholsterers, furniture restorers, conservators, historians and interior designers in Europe and America working together with the common aim of ensuring the care and maintenance of period and antique upholstery. All these groups have now recognized that such pieces represent a precious heritage, which must, as far as possible, be preserved. In the past, all these disciplines adopted a sensitive historic approach with the exception of upholstery, which was, for some reason,

overlooked. Perhaps this was due to a false assumption that period and antique upholstery could not be restored authentically and at the same time provide adequate comfort in use. As you will discover from the projects described in this book, nothing could be further from the truth. In fact, an elegant piece of traditionally upholstered seating has a very strong appeal, and can also be very comfortable.

Chairs, stools and sofas should always be regarded as functional household items which can expect to have a hard working life. Because of this, most of the materials used in upholstery have a relatively limited lifespan. It is this lifespan that we can influence and extend by using (and reusing) the best materials available, and by choosing the techniques most appropriate to the period and style of the piece being restored. The 'new-age' upholsterer should adopt an approach that combines restoration, conservation and reupholstery in equal measure, blending them all together in a sensitive and informed manner.

This book sets out to illustrate, by means of nine progressively complex projects, a wide range of traditional upholstery techniques, many of which, while initially learned on something simple like the desk chair in Chapter 1, can be applied to something far more involved, such as the chaise longue in Chapter 9.

Basic techniques are of course repeated in many of the projects, but they are also *adapted* to suit the job in hand. When restoring pieces such as those tackled in this book, it is just this level of flexibility that the upholsterer needs to develop, and I hope that reading the projects that follow will help you to develop a similar approach in your own work.

The projects appear in an approximate order of difficulty, beginning with basic upholstery on small, manageable pieces and building up to more complex, larger items. However, it is a feature of the craft that, on occasion, while a small piece may at first appear an easy option, it turns out to be far more complex, and demands a very precise approach. A good example of this is the small back panel on a Victorian or Edwardian chair. Such panels often have to be upholstered into a shallow rebate, and have a fine stitched edge with a well in the centre. The Regency music stool in Chapter 2 has a similar type of upholstery.

Obtaining antique upholstery

In the trade, 'period' upholstery refers to pieces made before 1800, and 'antique' upholstery to pieces made during the nineteenth and early twentieth centuries.

I have deliberately chosen 'antique' pieces which combine points of interest with relative ease of availability, and as a result it is the period between the Regency (1811–1830) and the modern-day (1940–1960) which is covered by the projects. Upholstered pieces dating from the nineteenth and early twentieth centuries remain very popular, and are readily available to the upholsterer at affordable prices.

Pieces can often be found at car boot sales, auction sales (which have the benefit of being able to view pieces in advance of the sale), and, of course, antique shops. By this I do not mean the grander outlets, where everything has already been restored, but rather what might better be termed 'used furniture shops', who, along with run-of-the-mill items, frequently have unrestored pieces from the periods mentioned in their stocks – ideal for the upholsterer. Many such shops are run by a group of dealers and are more of a market than a shop, and such places are always worth a visit. Always remember that the type of piece you are looking for may not be on display, so always be prepared to ask – you never know what might be tucked away out of sight!

Other places to look are the large antique fairs which take place on a regular basis round the country, and country house sales, where items on sale from the host-house are often topped up with pieces from other houses, making the amount of furniture on sale considerable and the types of piece wide ranging.

Finally, make a point of telling friends, family acquaintances and colleagues that you are interested in upholstery. You may be surprised at what people have stored away in their lofts or garages, and very often this approach turns up some wonderful pieces in need of restoration.

Dating upholstery

You will see from the projects that the old upholstery of a piece is often an excellent indicator of its history, if you know what to look for, and you will often find that a piece has been reupholstered several times during its life, with a number of different coverings still in place. Webbings, lining cloths, hessians and stuffings will help to confirm that a piece was designed and manufactured during a specific period (you can usually narrow it down to within twenty-five years). For example, narrow webbings of 1¾in (44mm) wide or less are likely to be of English manufacture, and date from around 1760. Likewise, black and white webbings with a twill or herringbone weave and coloured thread running along their length are also most likely to be English. Wider webbings, fixed closely together on a frame, are typical of continental upholstery from around 1800, and are also likely to be plainer than their English counterparts and made from brown jute or flax.

If the upholstery linings and supporting cloths are made from linen, then a piece is likely to be early Victorian. Linen is easy to identify: it is finer and has a softer feel than the jute materials which superseded it, and turns a pale grey colour with age. Jute cloth, on the other

hand, becomes darker brown with age, and will also tend to be very brittle.

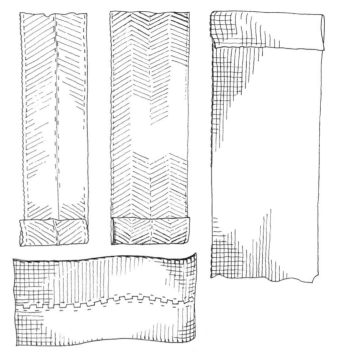

Identifying webbings. Clockwise from top: early English, dating from around 1760; English black and white herringbone weave; wide continental linen or jute; late Victorian jute.

You can also learn a lot from the type of spring used in a piece. Upholstery springs were first patented in the 1830s, but they were not used in large quantities until later in the Victorian period. Early springs (dating from around 1860) were quite heavy and crudely made, and their ends were bound and finished with fine wire (see Chapter 6 – the restoration of a mid-Victorian iron-back chair). Later examples (dating from around 1890) were machine-made, used a lighter gauge of wire and had a single knot, or turn, to finish their ends. Such springs were in turn superseded in around 1930 by springs made from spring steel with a double knot, machine twisted, to finish them.

3

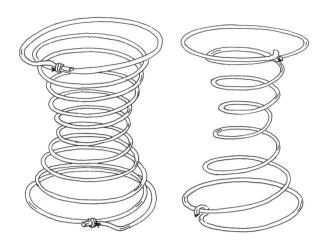

Identifying springs. Clockwise from top: early spring with wire-bound ends; late Victorian machine-made spring; modern spring (post 1930), machine-made with double twist knots.

Finally, dust and grime, broken frame work and well worn castors are all sure signs of age. Dust often emanates from the inside of the upholstery, where there has been a breakdown of materials, especially fillings such as seaweed (*Alva marina*), rag flock, wood wool, grass fibres, shoddy (wool waste) and cotton millpuff, all of which were used in quantity as fillings during the long period between 1880 and 1950. They were then gradually superseded by coir (coconut) fibre, Algerian black dyed fibre and latex rubber, in the form of foam or rubberized hair sheet. The use of such fillings was a significant development in the history of the craft,

and make it easier to date pieces in which they are found.

Tools

A wide range of hand tools are available to the upholsterer, and most students begin with the basic essentials and gradually add to these, building up their tools into a comprehensive kit. Many upholsterers (myself included) end up with at least two of everything. While it may seem extravagant, this can be extremely useful and cost-effective in the long run. For example, several pairs of scissors will prolong the life of each pair and save time during a job, as you won't have to have one pair resharpened in order to complete all the cutting operations required. Having at least two hammers is also advisable; one for heavy work, and one for lighter tasks.

You can never have too many needles for traditional upholstery work. Always keep a good selection of curved and straight types to cover all eventualities, from the smallest 2½in (64mm) curved cording needle to the large 18in (457mm) two-point straight bayonet needle. Using the right needle for the job is very important – it ensures good needlework, and also helps to prevent sore fingers.

All the tools shown on page 5 were used at some stage or another in the restoration of the pieces featured in this book, along with an industrial sewing machine fitted with a plain presser foot. This was changed to a piping foot to make the cushion covers for the pieces restored in Chapter 4 and Chapter 9.

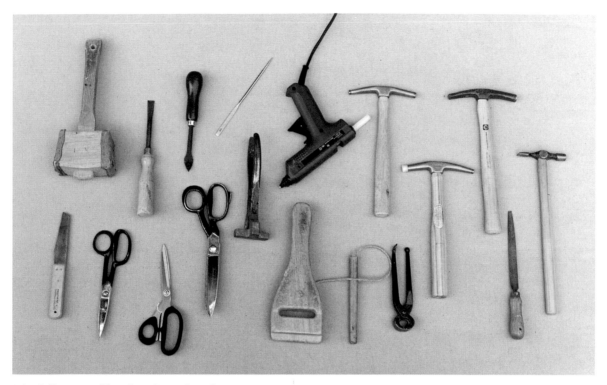

The full range of hand tools used in the restoration projects.

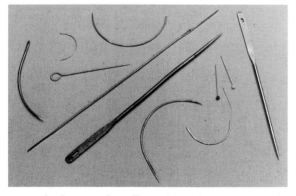

A good selection of needles and regulators is essential.

Removing old upholstery

Removing the upholstery from a piece of antique furniture requires care and consideration. However, you can always avoid damage to the delicate framework and the show wood as long as you use the correct tools. Always remember that timber can become dry and brittle with age, particularly at the edges and along rebates and curves. Therefore, ripping-out techniques need to be adapted to each individual piece. Always use a good, sharp ripping chisel, along with the obligatory wooden mallet, a pair of pincers or snips, and a purpose-made staple remover. Try to avoid stripping with the ripping chisel across the grain of a rail or block of wood which are vulnerable and likely to split, and remember to support delicate tacking and stuffing rails during stripping and reupholstery, as otherwise they are likely to fracture or move.

I hope that the projects that follow will broaden your experience and understanding of the restoration process. I also hope you will enjoy, as I have, discovering and applying the techniques used by the craftsmen of the past, and that your work is enriched as a result.

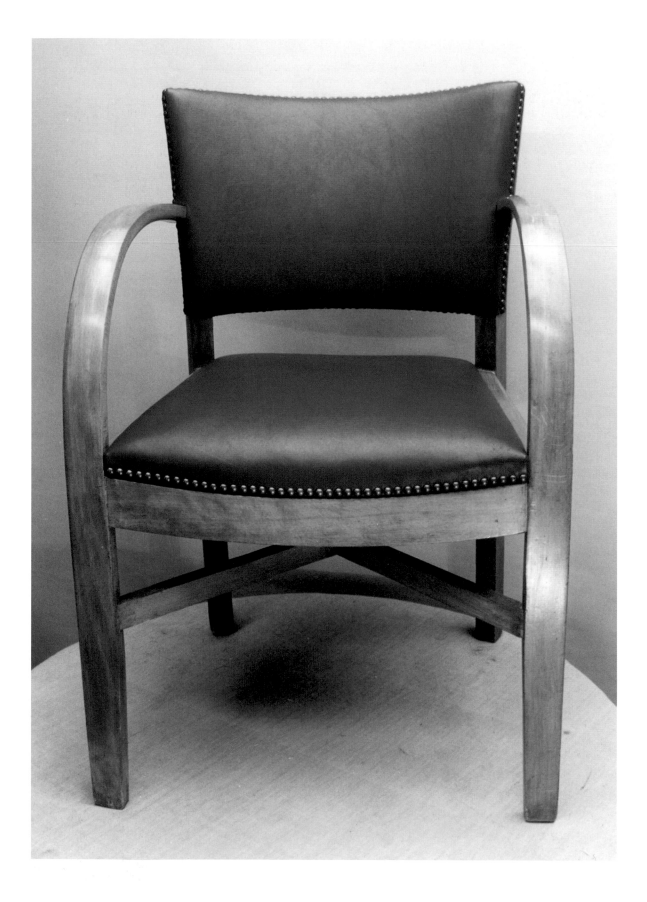

1 1950s desk chair with loose seat in leather

This chair is made entirely from beech, and the arms, as you can see, are single pieces of this wood, bent to shape. Chairs with long, bending curves as part of their design were quite common during the first half of the twentieth century. Similar designs were first produced in 1932 and 1934, made from tubular steel.

Loose seats were originally introduced to the UK in the latter part of the seventeenth century from Holland, where they had been in common use since around 1680. The loose seat has become an enduring design feature, as demonstrated by its appearance on this far more modern piece.

When it came to me for reupholstery, the chair had been completely stripped

of its original upholstery, and had been in storage for some years. The original loose seat frame had become detached at some stage, and was lost.

The series of holes you can see in the back frame suggested that the original upholstery had been secured by means of brass nails, which also suggested that the original covering material was hide. In keeping with this, I chose a wine-coloured upholstery hide as the new covering, which would be finished in the same way.

COVERING USED
10 sq ft (0.93 sq metres)
of hide (7¾ sq ft of hide
plus 25% for waste).

The chair frame was in quite good condition and reasonably sound, having only one loose joint. This was corrected by removing the corner block, opening up the joint, cleaning it out and re-gluing it. The frame was then cleaned to remove odd splashes of paint, using fine wire wool, before thoroughly waxing the show wood. The new loose-seat frame you can see here was made using measurements taken from the inside seat rails, and paper templates of the curves of the front and back rails. The frame was dowel-jointed together and fitted by planing off the sides and back edges to leave a 3mm (⅛in) gap all round.

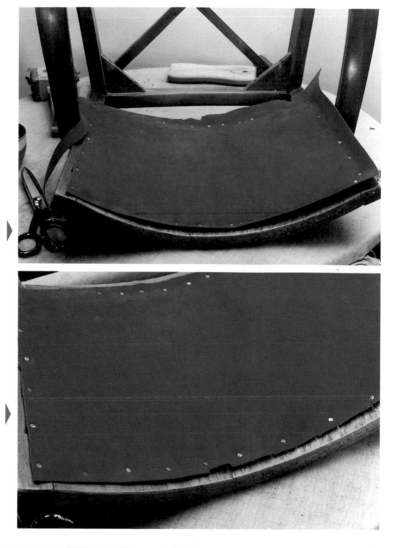

I began the reupholstery with the hide on the outside back, which was first tacked in place and then stretched by hand onto the frame. Stretching in this case was mainly done vertically, making the hide taut and ensuring it hugged the curve of the frame. This done, the excess was trimmed off.

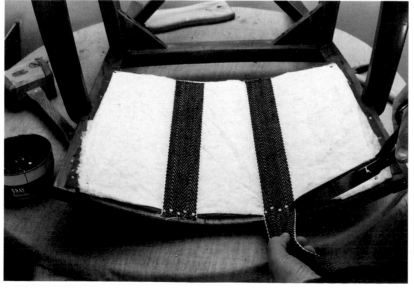

Next, a protective layer of skin wadding was laid over the hide and two vertical webs strained and fixed over the top. The webbing was tacked and trimmed without turnings to avoid unnecessary bulk.

A piece of 10oz
hessian was then
fitted over the webs
and tacked in place.

Ties were then sewn
onto the hessian using a
5in (127mm) curved
needle and No. 5 twine,
in readiness for a fairly
thin layer of curled hair,
which was tied in and
well teased. Always take
care not to overfill back
upholstery of this type.

The curled hair was covered first with cotton felt, and then with calico, both shown here. ▶

▲ The calico was first attached with a row of temporary tacks at the base of the back.

▲ It was then stretched vertically and diagonally, and the arm cuts made before the sides were tacked in place.

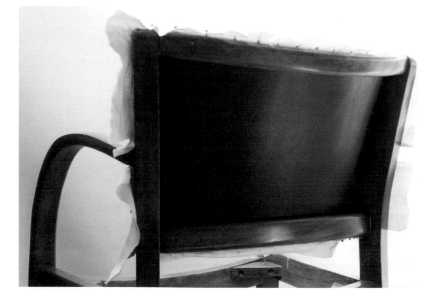

◀ Here you can see the calico set on and ready for final tacking off. Once this was done, I moved on to the next covering: the hide.

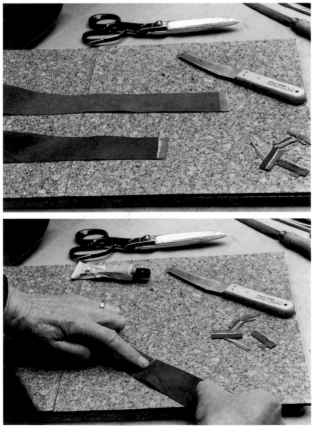

Because of the large waste factor which is always involved in cutting upholstery hide, and because upholstery hide is expensive, 'savings' are made by creating piping and banding strips made from the offcuts. The piping strips were 1½in (38mm) wide, and were joined together with a skived joint, whereby about ½in (13mm) is sliced off the face of one strip and the underside of the other. Here you can see a hide trimming knife being used to skive the piping ends, which were then glued together.

As you can see (or not!), once a strip has been machined up into piping, the joins will be virtually invisible. The piping cord should ideally be about ⅛in (3mm) in diameter for this kind of work. To avoid perforation when machine sewing hide, there should be no more than 10 stitches per inch (4 per centimetre). A guide to recommended stitch lengths for upholstery sewing is given on page 147.

Once created, the piping strip was tacked in place around the show-wood edge of the chair back. The ends of the piping were then trimmed and turned-in, to create a neat finish where they abut the arms on either side.

The back cover was then set on, and stretched in the same manner as the calico before it. Hide requires much firmer handling than calico, although it becomes more pliable and easier to work as it warms up with handling. You can see here the cuts I made around the edge, which are usually required in order to release tension in the hide as the stretching progresses.

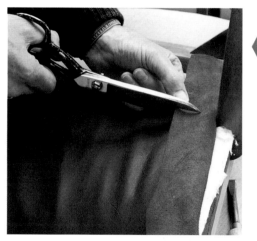

With the hide successfully set in place, cuts were made around the arms in a small 'v' formation, the width of the v being a fraction less than the thickness of the arm timber to allow a snug fit.

As the hide was smoothed and stretched a second time, red gimp pins were used to permanently fix the inner edge of the inside back. They would later be hidden by the brass nails (you can see the initial, temporary tacking to the left of the chair arm). The hide was then trimmed along the inside of the piping line, using a new knife blade for maximum sharpness. Always take great care at this stage not to cut into the piping.

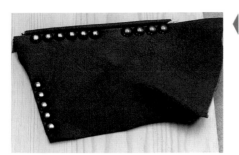

Before I began the nailing process, I made up a sample, using, (from left to right) bronze renaissance, antique on brass, and French natural nails, to see which appeared to be the most suitable for the chair. I chose antique on brass nails, and then needed to calculate the number of nails required. To do this, I measured the total length of the edges to be close-nailed, which gave me a distance of 170cm (68in). I normally calculate that close-nailing takes about three nails per inch (or three per 25mm), and this usually allows for a few extra which might be needed. Hence, I required approximately 200 nails.

The nails should cover the gimp pins that lie alongside the piping, creating a neat and elegant effect.

With the nailing completed, the back upholstery was finished. The next stage was the drop-in seat, and this began by webbing the new frame in a formation of three by three, as you can see here.

Next, a good dense layer of curled hair was tied in over 10oz hessian, to form the base stuffing.

Here you can see that the layers I used for the seat are exactly the same as those I used for the back upholstery – cotton felt, and then calico. The density of stuffings always varies in traditional upholstery work, and depends largely on the technique used to build the filling to the required height, feel and firmness. Stuffing ties with a good overlap are an essential part of the filling process, because as loose stuffing is pushed under them, they will flex and tighten, and hence the density is governed by the amount of stuffing under each individual tie.

A seat will normally require more filling, and to a greater density, than a chair back. For the seat of this chair, I used three handfuls of hair pushed under each tie, which produced a good, dense layer about 1½in (38mm) thick, all over the seat.

As with the back, once the filling was complete, the hair had to be picked and teased to give an even feel. This final operation is vital: it ensures you produce a seat that is free of lumps, hard areas, or soft hollows.

The calico lining was pulled down using temporary ⅜in (10mm) tacks, and well tensioned from back to front, so that the seat would retain its curve.

⅜in (10mm) tacks were then also used to set on the seat hide, which was then stretched in preparation for pulling down and pleating the corners.

The corners were then pleated, and as much hide as possible trimmed away, in order to avoid any excess build up at the corners.

Before the black bottom lining was attached, the seat was placed into the chair to check for a good fit, and four pilot holes were drilled into it to receive the four fixing screws. You can see one of these here, at the bottom right of the seat, with the hide cut away around it.

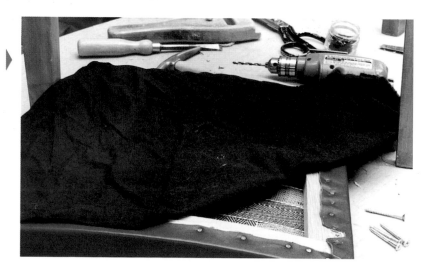

18

The completed seat with the bottom lining attached.

The completed chair, fully reupholstered and restored.

2 Regency music stool c.1835

An upholstered music stool of some description was part of the furnishings of most affluent households during the nineteenth and early twentieth centuries. This project is concerned with the restoration of a Regency music stool with an adjustable seat, c. 1835. A distinct feature of stools of this type is the turned and threaded mahogany centre column, which allows the seat height to be easily adjusted. The whole stool is made from this good quality mahogany, apart from the seat top, which is birch.

The reupholstery uses the traditional 'well-seat' technique. This creates a firm, well-supported, sharply defined stitched edge, and a deep second stuffing of curled hair.

The needlework cover was chosen for its suitability to the period and the style of the stool, and was bordered with a deep-coloured cotton velour. This treatment is typical of late eighteenth-century and early nineteenth-century upholstery, with plain but colourful borders creating a 'frame' around a piece of pictorial needlework tapestry.

Two other fabrics were in common use for such borders at that time: fine wool pile velveteens, and baize, which has a brushed wool surface. On this stool, the velour border was nicely complemented with upholstery cord and a scroll gimp.

COVERINGS USED

Needlework tapestry
350 x 350mm
(14 x 14in).
Cotton velour for the
border 100 x 125cm
(4 x 49in).

To begin, the old upholstery was completely removed. It was mainly rubber latex foam, which dated the last reupholster of the piece at some point during the 1950s. This done, the circular seat frame was cleaned up and lightly sanded.

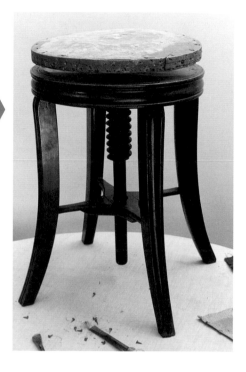

Here you can see the construction of the stool. The outer face edges of each leg are reeded, and the cross-over under-frame is cleverly braced to provide support for the central rotating column. The design is a pleasing combination of graceful lines and practical mechanics.

Furnishings were very often decorated with hand-made needlework during the first half of the nineteenth century. A small piece of seating such as a piano stool is an ideal candidate for this kind of needlework decoration, and so I chose a piece of attractive and colourful tapestry cut from an old cushion cover.

I chose a piece of deep-coloured velour with a fine cotton pile for the border surround, to match the needlework, along with trimmings of chair cord and a length of scroll gimp to bring the fabrics together.

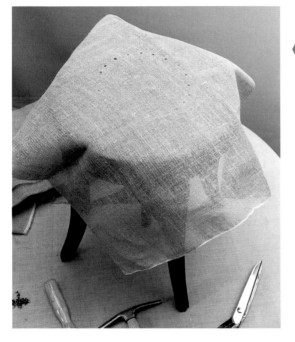

The 'well seat' type of upholstery is the most appropriate for this type of small stool, because it produces a firm built-up edge and a deep-filled centre that are independent of one another. Upholstery began with a large piece of linen scrim cut oversize by about 6in (152mm) all round. It was then centred on the seat with a circle of small fine tacks set about 3½in (89mm) in from the edge.

The scrim was then folded in while the stuffing ties were tacked and looped around the outer margin. The seat was now ready for the first stuffing of curled hair. An alternative to this would be a vegetable fibre filling such as curled coir.

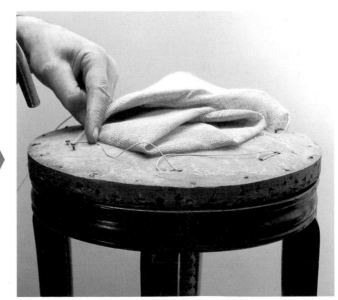

The first stuffing was then worked under the ties. Three small handfuls of hair were pushed under each tie to make a firm, dense edge about 2in (51mm) deep.

The strength and firmness of the filling was then tested by pulling the scrim out and over the stool and squeezing the filled edge. More hair was then added around the outer edge and the scrim pulled down and temporarily tacked onto the side of the stool.

The scrim was then trimmed and turned in, a small section at a time, and permanently tacked using ¼in (6mm) fine tacks. On round seats like this the scrim must be gathered and worked in, keeping the thread lines of the scrim vertical and not allowing them to drift too much to the left or right.

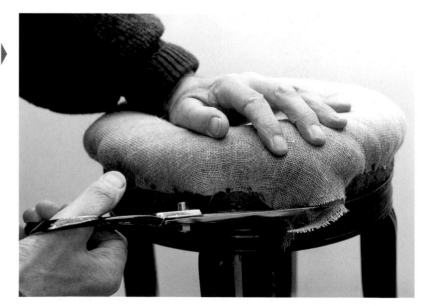

24

Here you can see the overall shape and outline of the first stuffing, which was improved by regulating the edges with a small 8in (203mm) regulator to keep them firm and even.

Because the edge was well filled, only one row of blind stitches and one of top stitches were needed to produce the shape and support required. Here you can see the blind stitch being worked around the seat just above the tack line with a two-point needle and no. 3 upholstery twine. On some seats more than one row of stitches will be needed – it all depends on the edge height required and the type and density of the filling. A very common combination is two rows of blind stitches and between one and three rows of top stitches.

A second length of no. 3 twine was then started off with a slip knot. The end of the first length was linked into it by twisting before tightening. This is a common method of attaching a fresh length of twine when the last one runs out.

25

Each length of twine was waxed before being stitched. This always helps to give twine a good grip and also reduces its tendency to twist, making stitching easier and more positive.

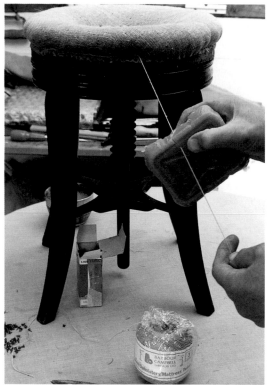

Next, the top stitch was sewn, using a 10in (254mm) two-point bayonette needle. This stitch sharpens and tightens the upper edge, and produces the final outline of the seat. It is important, therefore, that the stitching should be as even as possible, and parallel to the frame line.

A second, fairly dense, stuffing of curled hair was then tied into the well of the seat and built up to a crown above the edge line.

A layer of skin wadding was then trimmed to fit the seat top, which was now ready to be pulled down in calico.

The calico was initially set in place with four skewers, placed foursquare around the edge. It was then trimmed, turned in and skewered to the outer edge. It was then slip stitched to the scrim using waxed slipping thread and a 3in (76mm) circular needle.

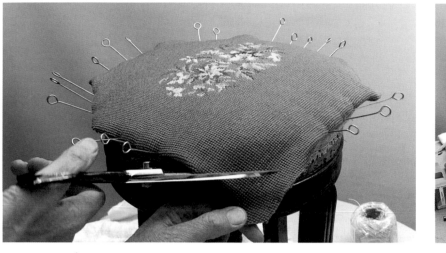

A second layer of wadding was then laid over the calico, and the cover trimmed, turned in and skewered to the edge. I was careful here to ensure that the floral design was set precisely in the middle of the seat top. Skewering the cover in place allowed for some final adjustments before final slip stitching took place.

The seat border was then filled using one thickness of 2½oz cotton felt and the cover set on with small pins and fine tacks, ready for stitching using a length of slipping thread taken from a plaited skein.

The seat edge was then masked with medium (8mm) upholstery cord, which was lightly twisted to ensure tightness and slip stitched onto the join. The two ends of the cord were sealed with sticky tape and trimmed before being tucked down together into the border joint. A few stitches were then made to pull the cord ends together and close the butt join.

Before the gimp decoration was applied the border velour was given a final trim to ensure that the underside of the seat top was completely free of upholstery.

I used a scroll gimp on this stool, which was first back tacked using two black gimp pins before being glued around the edge using a hot melt glue gun. The gimp served to seal the edge of the velour and enhance and decorate the seat.

29

3 Victorian salon chair with deep, buttoned seat c.1870

This attractive piece is one of a set of six inlaid salon or drawing room chairs, made from walnut. The chair is quite small, with a large amount of surface decoration, and when it came to me for reupholstery, the frame had been carefully restored. Some missing inlay had been replaced before the surface was cleaned, revived, and, where necessary, coloured to match the original wood.

Damage to the main seat rails (caused by tacking) had been repaired. The inlay on this piece is particularly fine, as you can see. It has aged beautifully and has a good patina. The main timbers used for the inlay here are burr walnut and boxwood.

Salon chairs from this period were mainly unsprung, and would have had either plain or buttoned seats with bordered edges, which were finished and decorated either by ruching (gathering) the fabric, brass nailing, or by adding upholstery braids or gimps. I chose to reupholster the chair with a deep, buttoned seat rather than a plain one. Such seats are extremely elegant, and introduce a number of interesting upholstery techniques.

Here you can see the chair frame with all its old upholstery removed, and draped over it is the green damask upholstery weave I chose as the covering.

COVERING USED

600mm (45in) of 127cm (50in) wide jacquard upholstery weave, plus 100mm (4in) for the plain border.

Here you can see some of the repairs to the frame that were required before reupholstery could begin. Beech had been used to repair the leg corners and the seat rails, and the damage caused by tacking was repaired by means of an injection of a mixture of glue and sawdust.

First, the seat was webbed using English 2in (51mm) webbing attached to the rails using 13mm fine tacks in a three-by-three formation. Chairs of this age require a delicate approach at this stage, because of the fragility of the frame. Always use fine tacks, and in areas where the frame is particularly worn or fragile, use 16mm staples instead. Once the webbing was firmly secured, a 10oz jute hessian was placed over it to form the seat foundation.

Here you can see the first stuffing of coir fibre being tied in and compressed along the ties to produce a good density of filling. This is especially important at the seat's outer edges, to ensure a firm edge ready for stitching.

A 7oz scrim covering was then set on the fibre, using 10mm fine temporary tacks, beginning at the back of the seat, and pulling forward to the front.

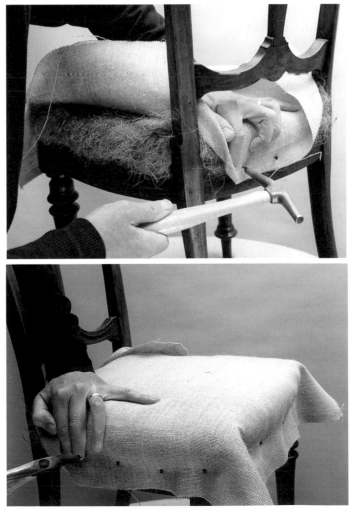

The scrim was
then cut diagonally
at the back legs,
and the excess
trimmed away
before the scrim
was tucked down
around the legs
using a regulator.

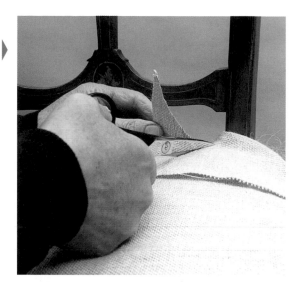

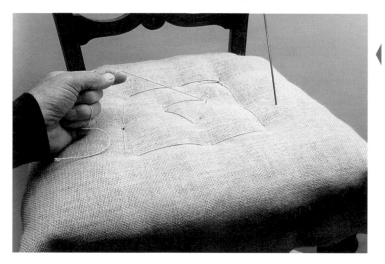

Once the scrim was tightly in
place, the bridle stitches were
put in, running down through
the seat and then tightened
down before being tied off. The
bridle stitches serve to gently
compress the seat stuffing, and
help to stabilize the whole of
the centre area, ready for the
work required on the edges.

Here you can see the
shape and outline of
the seat and its
edges, and the scrim
in the process of
being trimmed,
turned in, and
tacked onto the rail
edge chamfer.

Now the edge stitching could begin. Here I have started to build the stitched edges, using a regulator to ensure the edge is even and achieves a firm, full shape. The first row of stitches was a blind stitch using a two-point needle and a no. 3 twine. You can see that this first stitch runs along the base of the edge just above the tacks, and already the seat has begun to change shape and become firmer.

When the corner was reached, the needle was pivoted from a centre point as the blind stitch was worked round the corner to the front of the chair.

The seat required a second row of blind stitching to sufficiently firm-up the edge and create a good foundation for the subsequent rows of top stitching. Here, you can see the first of the two top stitches in place. At this point, the sharpened edge should always be regulated to help maintain shape and firmness.

As with the music stool project in Chapter 2, the stitching twine was waxed by drawing it through a block of beeswax to strengthen it and take out some of the twist, making it easier to handle. Waxed twine is also less likely to fracture any material through which it is drawn, so, although this is an optional process, I thoroughly recommend it.

Here you can see the completed stitched edges of the seat, with both rows of top stitching in place. The seat is now a good shape, and follows the frame line well. The sharp edge line is ideal for any seat which is destined to be bordered, as this is.

The next stage was the buttoning of the seat. I chose a four-three-two (front to back) formation, which I initially laid out with large tacks and the aid of a tape measure. This formation is very typical of buttoned seats, and is also extremely suitable for a seat such as this, which 'tapers' to a narrow back.

Holes were then cut in the scrim at each button position, with vertical and horizontal cuts radiating from each, to allow each button and its surrounding fabric to sink in to a good depth. This done, the stuffing in each hole was cleared out, also to a good depth. The best tool for this job is your fingers!

The position for each button was then transferred to the bottom of the seat, by passing a needle (or a regulator) through to the webbing, and marking each position permanently with a felt-tip pen.

Once the button marking was complete, the second stuffing of curled hair was well teased and then tied in. At this stage, always make sure the stuffing ties do not pass over the buttoning holes, but instead run along between so as not to obstruct them. Then a thick, soft topping of cotton felt was laid over the stuffing and trimmed to the seat shape. The seat was then ready for buttoning.

37

Here you can see the chosen covering in detail, along with the matching, deep-green upholstery cord and the multi-coloured coronation braid, which I chose to blend with the colour of the walnut frame and enhance the seat-edge line.

First, the fabric was laid face-down, and the buttoning pattern marked on the reverse. Always begin by drawing the centre line (shown clearly here), and then marking out from it as a guide. The size of the diamonds was increased on the fabric by 1¼in (32mm), so that they measured 9¼ x 5¼in (232 x 133mm), whereas those on the chair measured 8 x 4in (203 x 102mm). This allowed sufficient fabric to successfully deep-button, and also create a pleated effect where the fabric descends into each button hole.

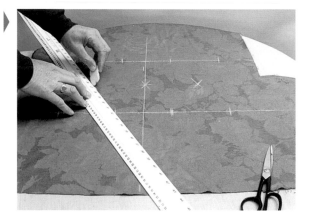

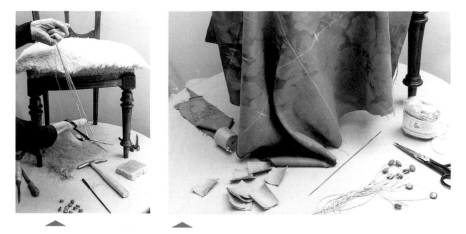

You will find the buttoning process proceeds much more smoothly if you ensure that all the materials and equipment needed are easily to hand before you begin. Prepare the buttons by threading them onto pre-cut, identical lengths of twine, as shown here. In addition, cut out some small pieces of webbing or fabric such as those shown on the right, which can easily be rolled up to make the toggles used to hold the button twines under the seat. I chose a smaller button size than normal for this chair (22 rather than 24) as this seemed more in keeping with the chair's size and delicacy.

First, a 10in (254mm) two-point needle was pushed up through the stuffing from under the seat at the centre button position. This is always the starting point for buttoning. A hole was then carefully made in the cotton felt, and the needle located through the centre position on the fabric.

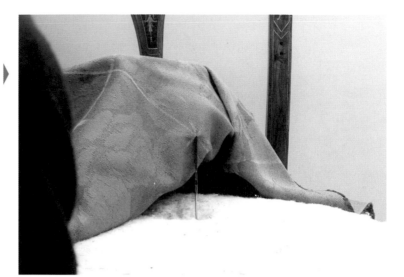

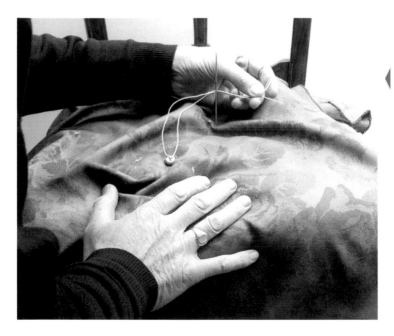

Both ends of the twine were then threaded, and the needle pulled sharply down through the seat. Before tying off the button, both button and fabric were eased down to half-depth in the seat stuffing, by pushing the button down from above, at the same time pulling the twine.

A slip knot was then made in the twine, and a webbing toggle placed into the loop. The twine was then pulled to hold the button at the half-depth position.

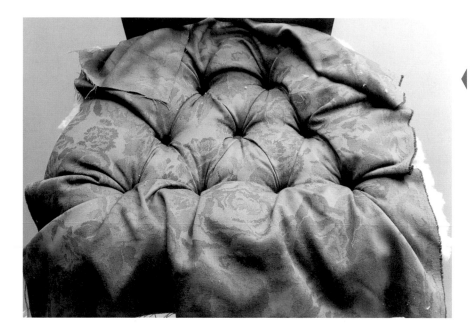

In this way, working out from the centre, all the buttons were pulled into the seat to half-depth, giving the top of the seat the appearance shown here.

Next, the cotton felt was carefully trimmed to produce a thin edge (I always use my fingers rather than a tool to do this), and tucked in under the hair. This leaves the stitched edge roll clear of felt and ready to receive the skewers which hold the pleated fabric.

I then carefully folded each diamond pleat using my fingers and a regulator so that all the pleats were laid to face towards the seat front. This serves to remove almost all the fullness before the outer, straight-edge pleats are skewered.

40

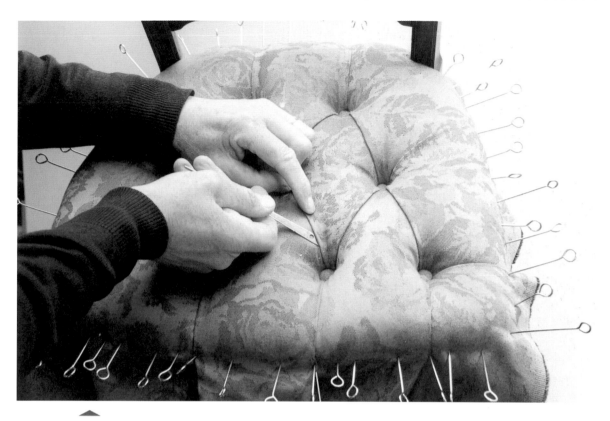

The buttons were then checked for position, and pulled a little deeper into the seat by adjusting the slip knots, and tightening each button down to an even depth. The diamond pleats must then be re-checked and neatened up using the fingers and a regulator, as shown here.

By working slowly round the seat, the edge fabric was trimmed off just outside the skewer line, and turned under to be refixed into the edge with long pins. The cover was then slip stitched permanently to the scrim edge roll using a 2½in (64mm) circular needle and a strong, matching thread.

Next, the border strips were pinned along the edge line. The edges were first filled with cotton felt (which you can just see poking out from the end of the covering), and then the covering fabric was tacked down over it, along the show-wood edge.

The borders were then slip stitched into the top edging, taking care to keep the stitching line straight, and as even as possible.

Once the stitching was finished, the border cover was permanently tacked down with small tacks (you could use gimp pins), and then trimmed off. All the button twine slip knots were then checked for tightness, and then tied off under the seat, and any excess trimmed off.

The final stage was to add the cord and braid, both of which have the function of being decorative, and also of covering up the stitching and tacking lines. A small, close slip stitch was used to fix the cord into the seat edge seam. As the stitching progressed, the cord was twisted a little to give a tight and even corded edge.

Finally, the braid was glued on around the show-wood line. I used matching gimp pins at the front-leg corners where mitring and folding of the braid was necessary.

4 Regency library chair with squab cushion c.1840

This is a strong and well proportioned chair, made at some time during the late Regency period, around 1840. Its design and definitive style incorporates some classical Regency features, such as the turned and carved front legs and the arm scrolls, which are very typical of the period. The caned seat was designed to be used with a reversible squab cushion, the upholstery of which is the subject of this project.

Chairs of this type are also known as bergère chairs, which were introduced to the UK from France around 1725, and at this time would have had upholstered backs and sides. However, these chairs are described by Sheraton in the *Cabinet Directory* of 1803 as having a caned back and bare arms, and this style, which is the subject of this project, also became quite common.

Here you can see the new caning being put into the seat. The new canework was stained to blend with what remained of the original canework.

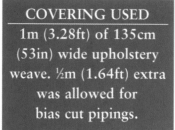

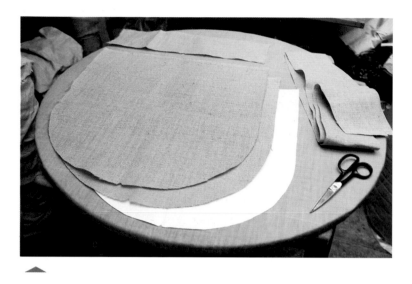

While the canework and frame of the chair were being
restored, a paper template was taken for the new, hair-
filled seat squab. To give the chair its correct seating
height, the squab needed to be about 3¼in (83mm) thick.
Cases for cushions of this kind can be made from cotton
ticking, cotton duck or a good jute or linen scrim.

The upholstery work began with the cushion parts being cut from a good 9oz jute
scrim. Allowances were made for the sewing and the making up, and ½in (13mm) of
material allowed to take account of the machine sewing required. A further 1in
(25mm) overall, or ½in (13mm) all round, was needed to compensate for the
reduction in size once the cushion was tufted and stitched. Here you can see the cut
parts ready for machine sewing, with the centre-back balance marks clearly visible,
although the pattern and scrim were also notched at the centre, front and back.

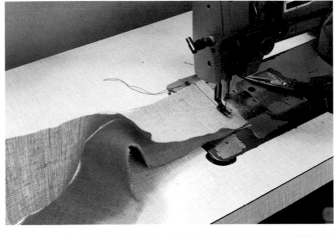

The machining sequence for making up the case: the two border pieces are joined together, and then sewn around the first panel.

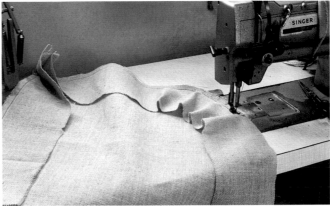

The top, or second, panel was only partly machined, in the form of a 'lid'. The corners were then trimmed before turning to allow clearance and make them neat and sharp.

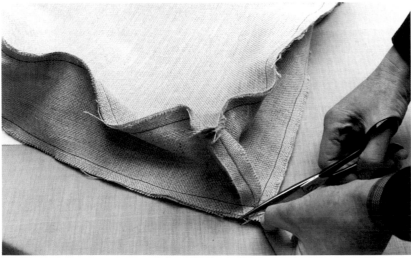

The completed case was then turned out, ready for filling with new, curled hair. When available, washed, reclaimed hair can be used, or can be blended with new hair, as you wish.

Filling the case began with small handfuls of evenly teased hair, pushed well into the front corners. Then the centre front was filled, and the sequence repeated, so that the left and right sides were pushed up to the level of the first layer, after which the centre was filled again, and so on. Controlling the height of the cushion and the density of the hair is very important, and is achieved using the free hand placed on the surface as the filling progresses, as shown.

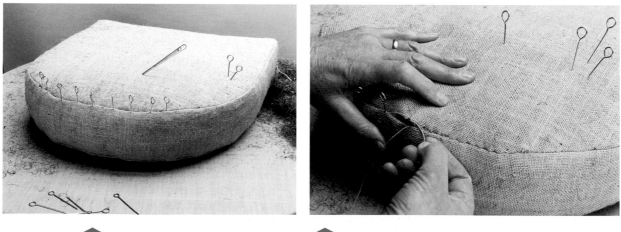

When the stuffing is firm and evenly packed throughout the cushion, the gap can be skewered and closed, using a waxed thread and a close slip stitch.

A regulator was then used to manipulate the hair filling in order to firm the edges by easing the hair out to the seams, on both sides of the squab. It is important to do this before, during and after edge stitching.

Once the case has been filled and closed the cushion can be weighed. The weight of similarly-sized cushions will always vary, depending on the density of the filling and the thickness of the cushion. However, it is also a good idea to note the size and the weight, as these will help with accurate costing in the future. This squab at 3¼in (83mm) thick, used 9.5lbs (4.3kg) of new curled hair.

The cushion can now be tufted. The technique of tufting is a very old one, with its origins in the early eighteenth century, used to hold out and set the thickness of cushions or mattresses. Tufts help to stabilize the cushion, and at the same time can be used to set the depth and feel of the interior. By compressing the centre tufts, a firm core can be created, in readiness for a deeper than normal second stuffing, which will be required for this cushion. The tufting arrangement is a series of adjustable ties set in a diamond formation, and tacks were used to mark out the tuft positions. The tacks can easily be moved around until a balanced and acceptable layout is achieved. The number of ties in this project is normal for this size of cushion, and left sufficient space between the outer tufts and the edge for the mattress stitching which followed.

The underside of the cushion was then pierced, causing the needle and twine to emerge from the surface, at which point a slip knot was made. Note that the two twines are set diagonally in the scrim, which gives a stronger fixing for the tuft, and is much less likely to tear the scrim yarns.

Here you can see the tufting twines, which should be left as slip knots so that they remain adjustable while the edge stitching takes place. This is important, as the edge stitching may change the shape and density of the hair filling, hence final adjustment of the tufts must be left until after the edge stitching is complete.

The first row of fine mattress stitches was then made, in a zig-zag, blind formation, drawing the filling outwards and making the edges firm.

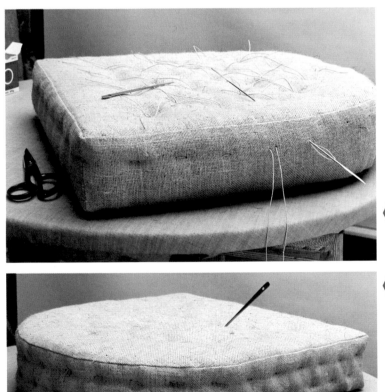

The cushion was then flipped over, and the same mattress stitch applied, but this time staggered between those made on the first side.

The mattress top stitch was then worked, at a rate of two stitches to each space between the blind rows. The top stitch should pierce right through the edge, and return at an angle to form the next stitch. All the stitches should begin with a slip knot, and be about 6mm (¼in) each in length. Continuous regulating during this phase will help to maintain a good, upright cushion edge.

The completed edge stitching, clearly showing the stitch pattern. ▶

◀ The tufting ties were then adjusted by tightening them down so that they were all the same depth, ensuring the surface of the cushion was flat, and then tied off.

A second stuffing of hair was then tied in, and evenly teased on both sides of the squab, to the depth required to produce a soft comfortable seat. The hair was then overlaid with a layer of wool or cotton felt.

Next, the calico case was made up to the template size, plus an extra ⅜in (10mm) for sewing allowance. The making-up sequence was the same as for the scrim case, except for the top panel, which could only be sewn part way round, to allow for filling.

The completed case was lined with a single thickness of felt, plus narrow strips along the inside of the borders.

The stitched squab was then eased carefully into the case, and topped with another layer of felt.

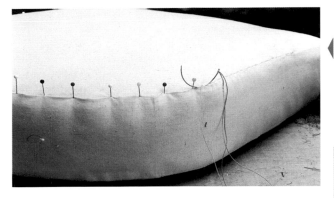

The calico case was then closed, and slip stitched using a 3in (76mm) circular needle and a fine thread.

The red and green upholstery weave chosen for the cushion was marked out using the same paper template as the inner covering, plus a 10mm (⅜in) sewing allowance.

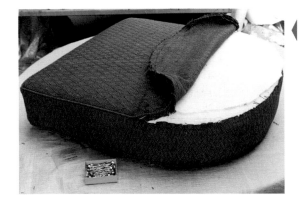

Two widths of the 135cm (53in) wide cover were then cut for the borders, and the joins set half-way along each side, rather than at the front corners, to make them less noticeable when the cushion is in use. The seams of the top and bottom panels were piped before assembly, although plain or corded seams would be equally appropriate to the period of the chair.

The cushion was completed by closing the case using a close slip-stitch applied to the inner edge of the piping.

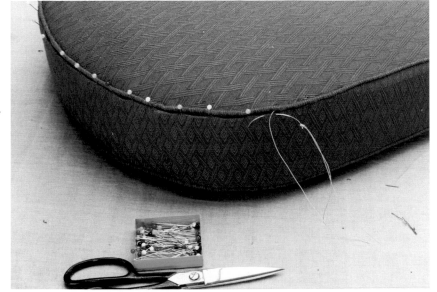

5 Victorian box ottoman c.1875

Box ottomans were produced in many different forms during the Victorian era, and sometimes had a dual function – as a storage space for household items (the nature of which depended on the size of the ottoman), and

as a seat. Long chest-like ottomans were commonly found in bedrooms, and used to store linen and other bedware, and were sometimes a fixture in the form of an upholstered

window seat. The smaller and more mobile examples, such as the ottoman which is the subject of this project, were used as work boxes and storage places for small items, typically the paraphernalia of sewing or needlework.

Ottomans originated in Turkey, and were first introduced into the UK at the end of the eighteenth century. They quickly became a fashionable furniture item, corner ottomans being made as cosy seats,

and round and octagonal ottomans made for the centre of rooms. Ottoman stools, boxes and chests were produced by Victorian craftsmen as low seats with (and sometimes without) storage areas below. In the catalogues of the time, they were often described as being 'wholly covered in stuffs' – in other words, completely upholstered pieces of furniture.

This project is a small ottoman of elegant design, supported on castors with a once-lockable lid. The box itself and the upholstery were in poor condition, with the softwood (pine) carcass in need of restoration. You can see from the photographs that two coverings and parts of two chintz linings were still in place, and that the original lid upholstery was partly collapsed. You can see that the lid had been covered in a red mohair velvet, which still retained some of its bright colouring.

COVERINGS USED
800mm (31½in) of
125cm (49in) cotton
print for the lining.
1m (39in) of upholstery
weave for the box.
20in (1.64ft) of velour
for the top.

None of the upholstery was reuseable, and so it was all carefully removed. The feet and the mahogany mouldings were unscrewed, allowing complete removal of the cover and the linings. The box itself was then cleaned and lightly sanded.

Here you can see all the parts removed from the box of the ottoman, including the hardware, the mouldings and the hollow-turned bun feet. The four mahogany mouldings were numbered at this stage to correspond with numbers on the box, so as to ensure that they were replaced in their original positions.

Removing the bottom of the box proved difficult, as it had been nailed in place, with two nails driven in from each side. Using pliers and a lot of patience so as to avoid damage to the box, the nails were eventually removed. Had the box been made from a hardwood, then the nails would have had to be sawn through using a hacksaw blade eased into the small gap between the side and base of the box, thus allowing the base to be removed.

Finally, the base was successfully removed! You can see its original chintz covering still in place at this stage.

Past attempts at fixing the coverings onto the box had caused the top edges to crumble. These were repaired by letting in new pieces of timber and gluing them in place, as you can see here. The hinge locations also required reinforcement.

I chose three fabrics for the reupholstery of the box and lid (from left to right): a cotton velvet for the lid; a matching upholstery weave for the outer covering; and a lightweight print for the lining.

First, the printed lining cloth was prepared and cut.

The upholstery then began by fitting and tacking the printed lining to the top and bottom edges of the ottoman. At each of the four corners the excess was snipped to a close fit and then turned in and gimp pinned with a matching colour about every 50mm (2in).

Once the lining was complete, the bottom board was covered, but, in the interests of conservation, the original chintz left in place as proof of the piece's age.

To reduce the risk of splitting the wood, the cloth was fixed with ½in (13mm) gimp pins, rather than tacks.

Once covered, the bottom board was relocated and screwed in place, so that anyone needing to dismantle the ottoman in the future would not have to contend with nails!

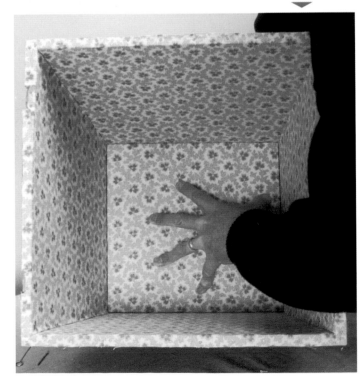

The original lid frame was in such a state of disrepair that I felt it was not worth restoring. Instead, I had a new lid made up from 15mm (⅝in) thick beech, dowel jointed with 10mm (⅜in) dowels, and having a champer around its top outer edges.

The new lid frame was then carefully fitted to the box.

Upholstery then continued with the outer covering, which was carefully cut so that all four sides were identical in pattern, allowing them to match reasonably well around the box. Each of the four sides was then back-tacked along the top edges.

The box sides were lightly padded with a half thickness of skin wadding, held in place with a few fine tacks.

At each of the top four corners, the cover was then carefully trimmed out and turned in to form a mitre.

As covering progressed, the lock and the hinges were replaced, and the cover cut and fitted around them.

The mitred corners were then pinned securely.

The outer covering was then completed by slip-stitching each of the four corners using a linen thread and a 75mm (3in) circular needle.

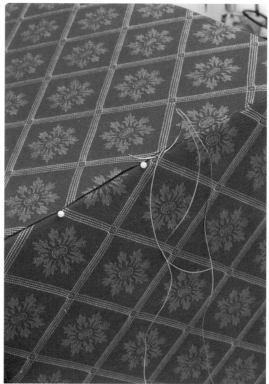

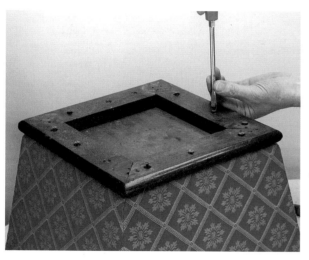

Next, the mahogany mouldings were replaced in their original positions and screwed down.

The mouldings were followed by the bun feet and the castors. The castors, which you can see clearly here, have two features of particular interest: the wheels are wooden, rather than metal, and are surprisingly well preserved, and the castor action rotates in a race, around a central pin within the bun foot.

Finally, the scuffs and scratches on the base mouldings were stained in, and a coat of wax applied to bring the show-wood back to life. This completed the box part of the ottoman.

I next moved on to the lid upholstery. Here you can see the new lid frame being prepared for upholstering. The sharp inner top edges were removed with a rasp, but could equally well have been scraped with a sharp knife. Note also the large chamfer on the top outer edge, created to facilitate the scrim tacking.

The frame was webbed in a three-by-three pattern using an 11lb, 2in (50mm) jute webbing.

It was then lined using 10oz hessian, tightly pulled over the webs.

The stuffing ties were then worked around the edge of the seat and across in one direction using a 5in (127mm) curved needle.

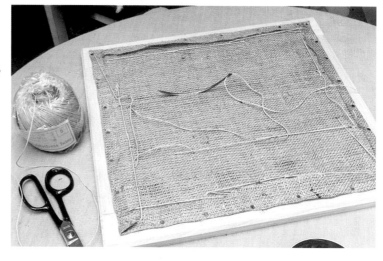

Next, new curled hog hair was tied in to a good density and a thickness of about 1½in (38mm).

A fine jute scrim was used to pull down the hair and form the upholstered shape of the lid. I used fine ¼in (6mm) temporary tacks to secure the first set-on, which was stretched very tightly as the edges were trimmed, turned in and tacked onto the chamfer.

The second stuffing consisted of one thickness of 2½oz cotton felt. It is vital that the felt is feathered off to produce thin edges around the tack line. At this stage it is important that all the scrim tacks are covered, in readiness for calico lining.

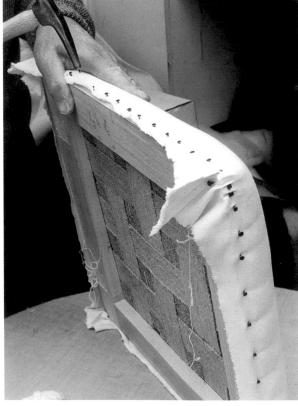

Like the jute scrim, the calico was pulled down tightly in order to maintain the curve of the upholstery. I used the fine ¼in (6mm) tacks again here to secure the calico, and made a very small pleat at each corner.

The lid was then checked for fit and shape before the covering began. Shape, form and proportion should all be checked at this stage, as they are vital to successful stuffed upholstery work. This is especially so when restoring period pieces.

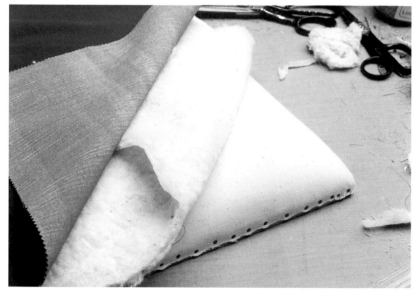

I gave the calico edge a final trim, and then overlaid the lid with a soft topping of skin wadding. This was trimmed to reach the tacking line, but not extend under the edge. I also cut the velvet cover to size at this point, which you can also see here.

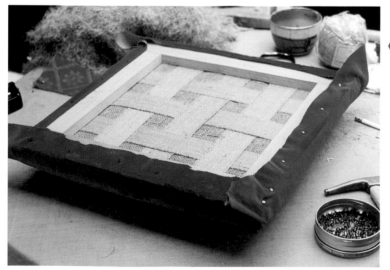

The velvet cover was then set on with temporary tacks. I always find that this is best done with the lid of the piece stood on its end, so that the grain of the cloth can be easily seen, and hence kept straight and square to the edges – very important if you want to achieve the most pleasing visual effect.

The corners of the cover were then set down and pulled very tight, before the excess was trimmed away and a single pleat made at each corner. Well-pulled corners ensure that lids such as this have a nicely 'rounded' appearance.

The lid was then re-hinged to the box.

The new printed lining was then pinned in place, ready for slip stitching. You can see that at this point I tacked a lifting tag made from 3in (75mm) cord to the centre-front of the lid. This should be done before the lining is fixed in place.

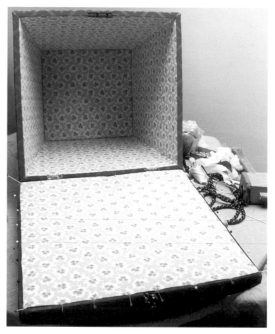

I used a hot-melt glue gun to fix a strip of decorative gimp around the edge of the box to enhance its appearance.

Further decoration in the form of some decorative cord was then slip stitched around the lower edge of the lid. The ends of the cord were bound and tucked into two small holes cut in the velvet.

The key tassel was made using warp and weft yarns taken from the box covering, mixed with some of the darker yarns from the unravelled upholstery cord used on the lid.

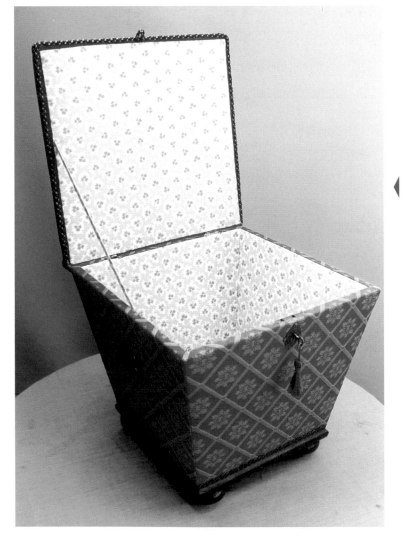

The completed ottoman. A length of the lining fabric was folded and machine sewn to form the stay, which was slotted in beneath the lining of the box and lid, and secured with gimp pins.

6 Mid-Victorian iron-back chair c.1860

The small size of this chair indicates that it was probably designed and made for use in a bedroom or a nursery. The seat is circular, and is supported on turned front legs with brass and china castors. The oval shaped frame back is made of iron, and is supported above the seat by three metal rods, which form part of the back construction.

The iron-back design was very common from the mid-Victorian period until the end of the nineteenth century. The malleability of the iron rods used to construct the frame allowed a freedom of design and style which hitherto had been restricted by conventional timber frame structures, and this in part gave rise to the distinctive shape of the back of chairs such as the one I chose for this project.

I bought the chair at auction for around £70, but you can also find them in antique shops and even junk shops on occasion, and they often turn up as part of a house clearance.

The chair's condition, though rather shaky, was fair, and perfectly restorable. The upholstery was a mixture of original and some more recent – and rather crude – coverings. Repairs were needed to the seat frame and to the right-hand front leg (as you look at the chair), which was listing badly.

To cover the seat and back, I chose a finely woven, rust-coloured tapestry fabric, with an all-over pattern, and matching cord and gimp. This was of course a personal choice of suitable material and pattern, and there are many

73

others that would be equally suitable for a chair of this kind. The material I chose has a slightly textured surface and a small, attractive pattern, which presented no danger of creating a distraction from the chair's inherently interesting upholstery design. In all, a 2m (6ft 6in) length of the fabric was required, being 140cm (55in) wide.

7½m (24ft 6in) of cord, and 2m (6ft 6in) of gimp allowed enough for the trimming with a little left over. The cording I chose was of the flanged type, which is a great help when locating and fixing the edge trimming. It is not, however, essential, and was in any case removed for the starburst pattern.

All the main tools and sundry materials needed for the covering work in this project are shown above, and are: scissors; a selection of hammers; a ripping chisel; pins; 3 and 4in skewers; a 2½in circular needle; a regulator; a 5in curved springing needle; a glue gun; cording (with and without the flange); slipping thread; hot-melt glue sticks, and replacement castors. The castors (two cup and two screw type) came from a stock of old hardware collected by a colleague who is a furniture restorer.

The coverings and trimmings I used are shown on the left.

Once the outer covering had been completely removed, the true history of the chair began to emerge. The upholstery design on the chair back is, as you can see, in the form of a starburst, created with 10 rows of yellow and red cording (removed at this stage), and the iron supports were also over-wound with the same decorative cord.

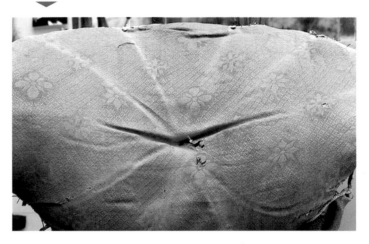

The chair seat shows the results of an amazing blend of techniques used in previous attempts to keep it functional, using a variety of webbings and tapes. A variety of upholstery grass stuffings were also used, and these can be seen stitched together around the outer edges of the seat.

Four large, and almost certainly original, seat springs were still in place, and can be seen clearly here with the chair completely stripped of its upholstery. The springs are of the type first used in sprung upholstered seats, using a very heavy wire, having lots of coils, and being finished with fine wire bindings.

The castors were removed, and the whole frame cleaned down in readiness for essential repairs.

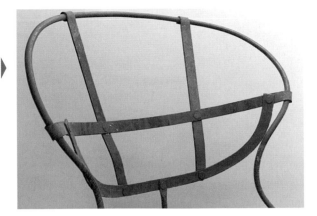

Here you can see the well-designed and constructed iron frame of the chair back. This has stood the test of time very well, and remains remarkably sound. The riveted and hammered laths were still tight, and the three supporting rods well formed and jointed, evidence of good engineering.

With the front frame joint eased apart, the two large nails holding the joint together were removed, and the broken dowels drilled out and replaced with new ones.

The complete seat was then reassembled, and cramped up overnight. The front leg could then be replaced, and reset in its true upright position.

Restoring the upholstery began with a 10oz hessian, used to line the back frame. This is the minimum weight of cloth for this type of work, but 12oz or 14oz cloth could be used instead. An overedge lockstitch secured the hessian to the outer rod, and an overhand stitch was made around the laths to hold the hessian to the frame. An alternative method, often used for lining-up iron frames, is to apply the hessian to the outer back face of the frame, and then stitch it in place in the same way.

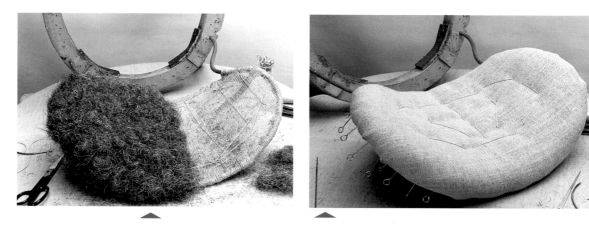

A good even thickness of curled hair was then strung onto the back of the chair as a first stuffing. This was then covered with a linen scrim, set with skewers, and bridled in place. The bridle stitches should follow the outline of the back frame shape.

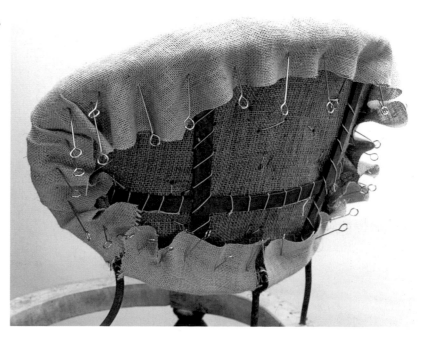

I then trimmed and
turned in the scrim,
before reskewering
once I had achieved
a good even
thickness of hair
added into the edge.

The outer rod was then completely wrapped in hair
and scrim before the top stitch was put in with a two-
point bayonette needle. At this stage I had to make a
choice: because the seat and the back upholstery were
separate, work could now either continue with second
stuffings and covering on the back, or this could be
left at the scrim stage and work on the seat begun. I
chose the latter course, but this was purely a matter
of personal preference, as it will be for you when you
come across a similar situation.

The seat was supported with eight 2in (51mm) black and white webs. The arrangement took into account the number of springs to be used in the seat, thus ensuring that there was adequate cushioning and support for the springs.

Six 5in (127mm) by 10 gauge springs were chosen, to give a medium-firm seat. Firmer support would be given by using six 9½ gauge or 9 gauge double cone springs.

The six springs were tied in using a three-knot formation (i.e. three knots to each spring in the pattern shown). The springs were then lashed to the webbing using a good laid cord, in a star formation, which always works well on a round seat.

A 10 or 12oz hessian was then pulled down over the springs and pulled taut, but not so much as to distort the springs or slacken the lashing. Each of the springs was then tied and knotted to the hessian cover three times.

The first stuffing of coir fibre could then be well built-up to a good density around the seat edge to a level of approximately 3in (76mm) to produce a level seat stuffing.

Here you can clearly see the seat level resulting from the stuffing, after the scrim has been set in place using ⅜in (10mm) fine tacks. Once set and reasonably taut, the scrim can be bridled in place. The bridle stitches that run parallel to the edge are deep running stitches, set approximately 5in (127mm) in from the edge. Take care not to catch the springs or the webbings with the bridles.

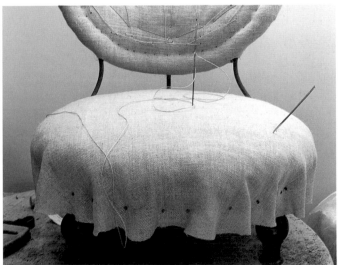

Once more stuffing had been added into the edge, the scrim was trimmed and turned, and permanent tacking begun along the rail chamfer.

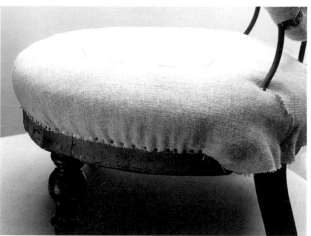

Because they have no corners, circular seats require some care in manipulating the fullness of the scrim, and should be worked in by gathering, *not* by pleating, as the tacking proceeds. This will ensure that the scrim line does not drift, and remains square.

The next stage was to form the stitched edge, with two rows of blind stitching followed by two rows of top stitching. This process should build the edge to about 3in (76mm) above the rail.

At this point I had to decide on what type of edge upholstery was needed. A soft, roll-over edge would need no further stitching, but this project had a bordered seat, and hence required a sharp and well-defined edge on which the calico and top cover would be sewn. To create this, a fifth row of stitching was required, commonly known as a 'feather edge'. This was formed using a knotted blanket stitch, worked closely round the top outer point of the stitched edge. This technique produces a strong and very firm foundation for the bordering work, as each stitch squeezes and sharpens the scrim as it is closely worked with an 8in (203mm) two-point needle.

Work then continued on the seat with a second stuffing of curled hair, tied in and built up to a soft attractive crown, which is both visually appealing and comfortable to sit on. The second stuffing was then pulled down in calico as shown here and skewered temporarily under the edge.

83

Once tightly set,
the calico was
trimmed and
turned in, as
refixing continued
along the edge.

The slip stitching
technique was
then used to
secure the calico
permanently. The
cuts to the metal
supports were
over-sewn to seal
them.

With all the upholstery foundation work complete,
covering the chair could begin, starting with the
inside back. The first stage was to mark the
starburst stitch lines onto the scrim foundation
using a soft pencil, and these can clearly be seen
here. This involved setting a centre point using the
original cover as a guide, and drawing radiating
lines out to the edge. Rather than repeat the
original ten-line pattern, I opted to reduce this to
eight, as ten seemed to me too visually crowded.

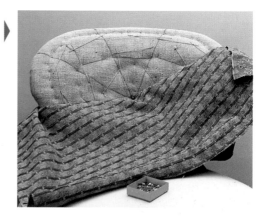

Here you can see the three bottom segments of the starburst filled with a very small amount of curled hair. A piece of cotton felt has also been inserted over the hair in each segment, having been cut exactly to size. The cover was then centred and pinned along the pencil lines, with a twine stitch pulled through the centre point to secure the cover.

This photograph shows the curled hair tied into the top left-hand segment, as filling progressed.

Filling and pinning then progressed around the back until all the segments were filled and set, by skewering over the edges.

Here you can see
clearly the lines of
running stitch
caught into the
scrim base, using a
3in (6mm) circular
needle and strong
linen thread.

Each piece of cord was
cut to length, sealed at
the ends with tape, and
tied into the centre with
a knotted thread pulled
through the centre
point, and tied off at
the back of the chair. To
reduce the cord size for
the starburst, and to
lessen the contrasting
blue colour, one blue
yarn was unwound and
removed from each of
the back cords.

The last cord (bottom right), was hand-stitched into a small rosette before being tightly sewn in place over all the cord ends. To complete the trimming, each cord was slip stitched in place along the lines of the running stitches.

The three supporting rods were then trimmed and, as a result, covered by overwinding them tightly with a fine matching cord.

This type of covering operation is effectively a repeat of the calico work completed earlier, with two layers of skin wadding laid and trimmed over the calico. Only a small amount of the fabric cover was turned in, so that a smooth line of slip stitching could secure the edge.

The flanged cord was then machine sewn to the border, which was then pinned in place and tightly slipped to the seat edge line.

A horizontal row of stuffing ties were used to hold the curled hair border filling in place. A layer of new cotton felt was then applied to complete the filling. Borders on Victorian chairs such as this need to be very well filled, so that a plump effect is created to give the seat its correct proportions.

With the chair laid face down, the border was tacked and finished, and the inside back cover stitched securely in place under the metal rod. A layer of thick cotton felt was then laid over the whole of the back frame – well padded outside coverings are essential on iron-backed chairs, so that the iron frame is well disguised.

The outside back was then pinned in place and closed with a close slip stitch.

The border cover was then carefully cut and gimp-pinned around each leg, before the black dust cover was fitted to the under-seat.

The chair was completed with the gimp fitted and glued around the seat edge. The gimp begins and finishes at a point close to one of the back legs.

7 1930s armchair with cane-edge seat

This is one of a pair of fully upholstered armchairs, made around 1930. Chairs of this type have a very distinct style of their own, with scroll arms and cane-edged cushion seats. An unusual feature is the turned mahogany front legs, which have brass castors, making them much more in keeping with the late Victorian period. The bun foot had largely replaced the turned foot when chairs such as this one were made, so it is reasonable to assume that the legs were fitted at the customer's request, as it was common for manufacturers to hold a stock of various foot designs to allow for customer preference.

This project concentrates wholly on the upholstery of the seat and, specifically, the construction of a traditional cane- or spring-edge, (the reason for which will become clear later). You can see the 'starting point' from which I began to work on the seat in the second photograph on page 92, with the back and arm upholstery already complete. Spring- or cane-edges were developed during the mid-Victorian period (1850–1870), and are frequently to be found in large, comfortable chairs and sofas of this and later periods. It is a fascinating, though labour intensive, technique, and was eventually superseded by the spring unit, around the time of the Second World War.

This project introduces two contemporary upholstery-fixing techniques and tools, which help to speed up the work: a staple gun which uses 10 and 16mm staples, and a Klinch-It tool with Klinch-It clips. The staple gun is one of the modern upholsterer's best friends, removing the need to use tacks and providing fast, efficient fixing for webbing and calico with the least amount of damage being caused to what may already be a delicate frame. The Klinch-It tool and its Klinch-It clips can be used as an alternative to the conventional method of stitching, for example, springs onto webbing. The clips have very sharp prongs, and are forced through the webbing and then turned flat by the action of the tool.

COVERINGS USED
3m (9.84ft) of 1.8m (72in) wide calico.
5.5m (18ft) of 130cm (51in) wide
linen velvet.

A deep-sprung seat of this type needs a suitably designed frame, so that the arrangement and depth of the springing is accommodated with all the rails in the right places. For example, the space between the seat rails and the tacking rails above them needs to be at least 102mm (4in). The front seat rail should be of a good height, and some additional support provided for the front row of springs. You can see that the project chair has an extra front rail fitted for this purpose. This is laid flat, and fitted between the arm uprights, to form a perfect platform for the spring edge. An alternative method, which is often used, is to have a slightly higher main rail, with an extra strip screwed and glued to the inside edge. There are no distinct advantages to either method, and which is used is very much a matter of personal preference.

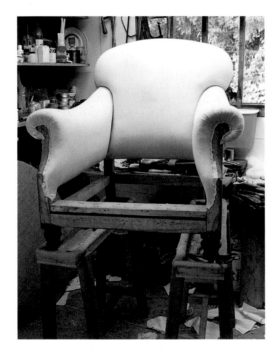

To begin with, English black and white 2in (51mm) webbings were fixed in place using 16mm (⅝in) staples. Seven or eight staples were required for each webbing, giving the equivalent of five tacks. The webbing layout was arranged to suit the nine 7in (178mm) x 9½ gauge main seat springs – that is to say, in three pairs running from the front to the back of the seat.

All the springs were then loose-laid into the seat, including the four at the front edge, as a check on their final arrangement, but were not fixed at this stage.

With the front edge springs removed, the nine seat springs were fixed to the webbing using Klinch-It clips and the Klinch-It tool. Three clips were used to hold each spring in place.

A strip of jute webbing was then laid and tacked along the top of the front rail. This provides a soft seating for the edge springs, and makes sure that, in use, there will be no unwanted noises or squeaks. Spring lashing then began, using two large ⅝in (16mm) improved tacks set at the end of each row of springs.

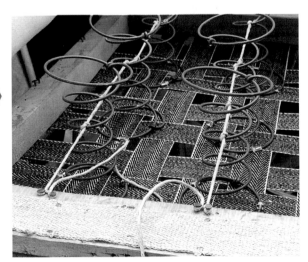

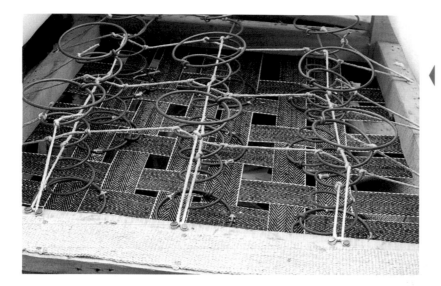

The nine main seat springs were kept upright by centre lashing the rows in both directions. This ensured a flat top to the seat, and aligned the springs with the front edge springs which were attached next.

Here you can see edge springs set along the front rail. These were fixed in place with a second layer of jute webbing and plenty of ⅝in (16mm) improved tacks.

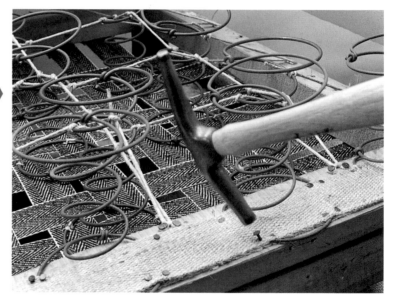

The springs were then independently lashed with a double length of good twine. Each spring was slightly compressed and set forward, level with the rail front. Their height is approximately equal to the main seat springs. Lashing began, by looping doubled twine around the inside base of each spring.

A piece of cane was then cut to length, and bent to fit exactly to the perimeter of the front seat-springs, with a return at each end. The return is achieved by 'notching' the cane, or by making a few fine saw cuts at each corner bend.

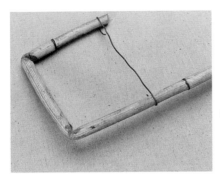

Notching involves cutting (using a fine saw) or filing away a 90° notch, which will allow the cane to be bent to shape. The cane should then be immersed in boiling water for 20 minutes to soften it.

The pre-formed cane was then lashed in place to form a strong and flexible spring edge. Lashing at each spring began with a metre length of good twine, doubled and looped around the spring and the cane, as shown. You will find that about 1in (25mm) of lashing will be needed at each fixing point.

The completed sprung seat is now ready for its first covering of 12oz hessian.

A gutter was formed between the front and second row of springs, by pushing the hessian well down behind the front row. The hessian was held in place with a length of cord and a row of stab stitches to the back of the seat rail.

The hessian was then lock-stitched in place and the first stuffing of coir fibre tied in, with the gutter well filled.

The first stuffing was then settled into place with a heavy weight, and left overnight.

Next, a good quality jute scrim was measured and cut, and then tucked in around the seat. The front edge was skewered under the cane with 3in (76mm) skewers.

The main cuts to the jute scrim were then made at each back corner, and behind the two arm uprights.

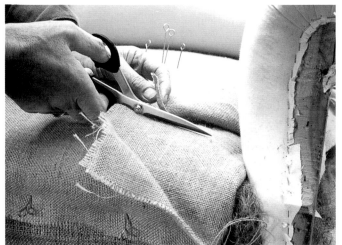

After the scrim had been pulled down and temporarily tacked, the pleated corners were made.

97

The seat was then bridled, to stabilize it and compress the first stuffing in place.

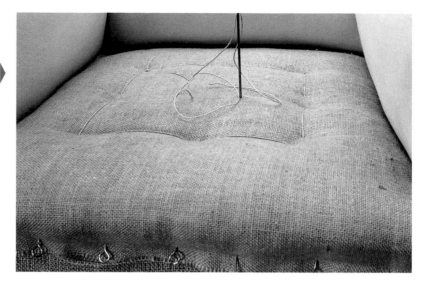

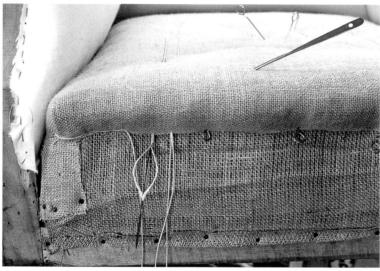

Now the stitched edge could be formed. You can see here the first row of stitching, for which I used a blind stitch to fix the scrim under the edge. This has the dual purpose of firming the edge as the folded scrim is also held permanently along the cane as a result. Remember to use the regulator before and during stitching, in order to ensure a strong and well-filled edge.

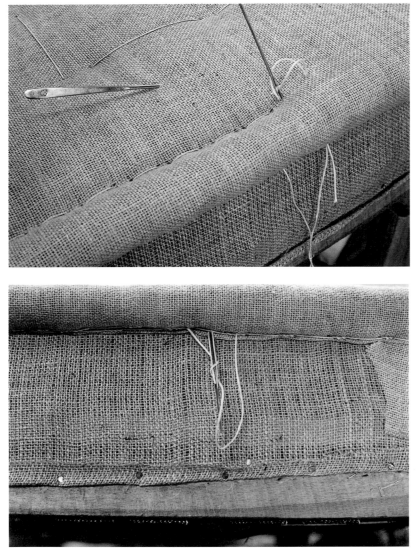

Here you can see the large, evenly spaced top stitch in progress, which forms the roll edge. The top stitch runs along the top of the cane, squeezing the scrim and first stuffing into a firm, well-formed roll. Two winds of twine, anti-clockwise around the needle, form the top stitch knot. This was then worked along the same line as the blind stitch.

Secure tacking-off is very important, as it ensures that the seat front and subsequent border stuffing are tight and well-supported.

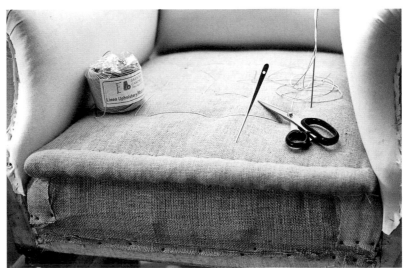

99

Always make sure the
materials are trimmed
and folded before
tacking once again.

A good layer of new curled
hair was then tied in, to form
the second stuffing. Always
make sure the tuckaways
around the seat are well filled,
as they are here. The seat was
then lined and pulled down in
calico, with the corners
pleated and skewered in place.

You can see that at each
front corner, the calico
end flaps are tacked to
the seat front rail.

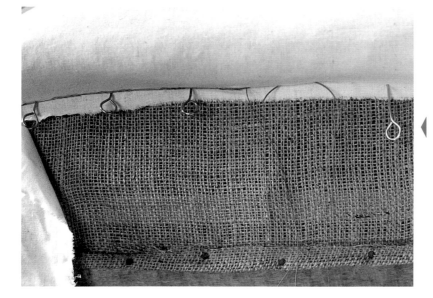

A 3 or 4in (76 or 102mm) circular needle was used to form the under-edge, and hold the calico before trimming off.

This completed the spring-edge element of the seat. This chair was one of a pair, and once both seats were complete, they were then brought up to calico, ready for the final covering, and the end result can be seen here. You can see that these sprung seats are quite low; this is on purpose to allow for the depth of two new feather-filled cushions.

8 Arts and Crafts armchair c.1900

The subject of this project is one of a matching pair of upright armchairs, upholstered onto an oak frame. It is an excellent example of the way in which the history of a piece of furniture is often revealed by the process of its restoration and reupholstery. It is always fascinating to find evidence of the materials and coverings which were in fashion and common use when a piece was first designed and made.

The style of this chair is typical of the period, and very similar to much of the furniture produced by Ernest Gimson and Edward Barnsley during the early years of the twentieth century. The 'Arts and Crafts' movement, begun by William Morris

in 1880, was perpetuated by these men along with other furniture makers such as Voysey and Russell. The style is, as you can see, relatively plain and unadorned, and this chair is constructed from oak, which was a very popular wood among the exponents of Arts and Crafts design. The simple carvings of natural forms on the arms and back are very 'craft' inspired and quite typical. This is a well-made and robust example, with turned front legs.

First inspection revealed the upholstery to be in reasonable condition. You can see that spaced brass nails and banding were used throughout to finish the upholstery, and the leathercloth covering was well-used but in quite good condition considering its age. You can also see in the close-up of the seat and arm that the coating of the cloth has become brittle from years of use, and this has resulted in the flaking you can see on the seat. Leathercloth, also known as American cloth or Rexine (which was a trade name), became very popular for use on domestic and 'club' furniture (literally, furniture designed for use in gentleman's clubs), from about 1900 until the Festival of Britain in 1951, which brought about an explosion of new designs and materials. Leathercloth was made from cotton cloth which was coated with nitro-cellulose and embossed and grained to simulate leather. The same material was used to line desk tops and table tops where a protective but elegant surface was required.

Here you can see the chair

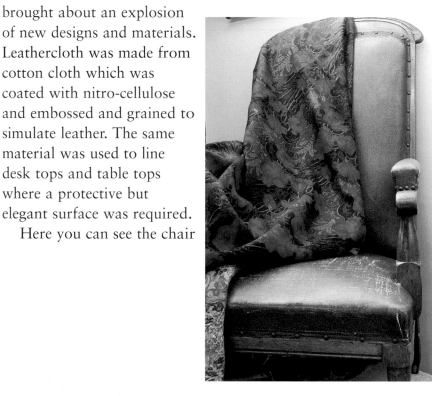

set on my workshop bench with a length of the new covering draped over the frame. Although in this case the fabric was chosen by the client, on those occasions when the choice is your own, draping a large sample over a chair in this way can make the often difficult choice of fabric or covering much easier. The design and colour of the chosen fabric should ideally relate to the size and proportions of the chair concerned, and also to the colour of the timber. The fabric chosen was an upholstery weight linen/cotton union, with a small percentage of nylon in its composition. The fabric was 127cm (50in) wide.

COVERING USED
2.5m (8.2ft) of 127cm (50in) wide floral printed union.

First, the seat and back of the chair were carefully 'ripped' using a ripping chisel and mallet. The process takes place in the reverse order that the chair was built, i.e. the under-seat dust cover and the outside back cover are taken off first, followed by the inside back and the seat covers.

Here you can see the upholstery construction of the seat, and the fillings of grass fibre and rag flock, certainly original, as such materials were banned from use post-1953. The large number of tack holes along the seat rails indicate that this seat has been re-webbed several times. Note that the seat has been 'boxed up': extra softwood rails have been nailed to the main seat to add height. This would have resulted in savings in materials and labour costs, as the seat could be upholstered quickly, using a small edge roll or dug roll, rather than needing a traditional stitched edge.

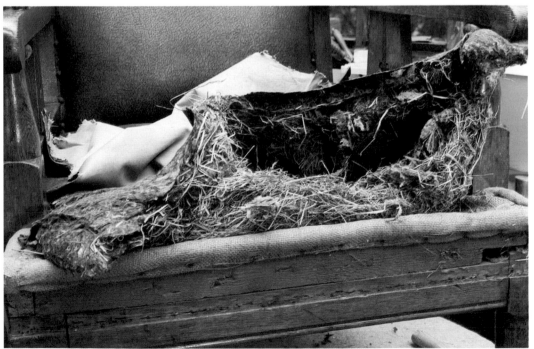

The back upholstery was supported by two webs, again original, along with an amazing mixture of crude hessian and canvas. The webbing design and weave is always good evidence or originality.

The old upholstery was cleared away and the workshop floor swept clean of tacks and other debris. The frame was then placed on the level floor, allowing me to check for any rickety, dry or broken joints. I then had these attended to by a furniture restorer, who, as you can see, also added two new beech blocks, which were screwed and glued into place on the inside corners of the seat and back joints. These serve to brace and strengthen the frame at its vulnerable points.

The 'level floor check' also revealed excessive movement in the front arm stumps. These were strengthened by drilling, and inserting 10mm (⅜in) dowels up through the seat rails and into the stumps. As the dowels were hammered in, fresh glue was forced into the arm stump joints. When the frame restoration was complete, all the show-wood surfaces were cleaned with white spirit and the frame revived with button polish. When thoroughly dry, the surfaces were waxed and polished, giving the show-wood a fresh lustre and enhancing the patina of the mature timber.

Rebuilding the seat began with a good web foundation using 2in (51mm) English webbing. Sprung seats of this size depend on plenty of webbing for support. An arrangement of seven webs (from side to side) and five webs (from front to back) was used, and the webs carefully arranged to suit the layout of the nine springs. I chose to use one more spring than the chair had originally because this is a far more common number, and makes subsequent work, such as the lashing, much easier. The webbing should always be strained tight in all directions, and interwoven, as shown. When straining against the show-wood, make sure the end of the web-strainer is padded with hide or wadding to prevent any damage to the wood, as you can see I have done here.

Here you can see that I kept the folded edges of the webbing well back from the rail edge, to prevent them being visible when the chair is stood down.

13mm (½in) or 16mm (⅝in) improved tacks were needed to securely attach the webbing to the frame on a seat of this size, and I used a three and two formation. Metal jaw strainers are very useful when fixing end pieces of webbing which are just long enough for the job, but would otherwise be wasted. They are also very useful when adjustments need to be made. The nine springs were arranged in three rows of three, and equally spaced. The springs I used were 6in (152mm) high by 9½ gauge. 10 gauge springs would also be suitable, but would produce a slightly softer seat.

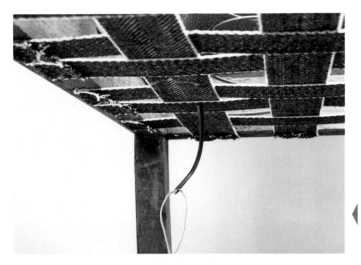

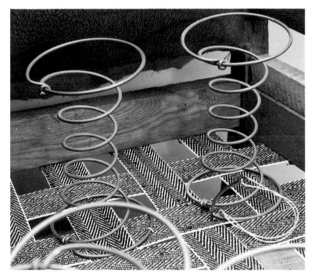

Tying the springs began in a back corner of the seat, with the springing needle piercing the webbing from below. The needle travels over the spring wire, and down underneath, to be knotted under the seat.

Each spring was then tied and knotted three times, in the continuous formation shown.

With the springs securely in place, but before lashing, a new edge roll was required along the front of the seat. I made this with a strip of hessian 5in (127mm) wide, close-tacked to the outer edge. Ready-made compressed paper dugging was then rolled up tightly in the hessian, and tacked down with ½in (13mm) fine tacks, at a slight angle to hold the edge roll firmly to the outer edge of the seat.

With the edge roll in place, the first stages of spring lashing could begin. A good quality laid cord was secured with ⅝in (16mm) improved tacks or clout nails. Lashing commenced at the back of the seat, with each spring knotted and tensioned down by a small amount. Take care to keep the springs standing upright and equally spaced throughout this procedure.

Here you can see the spring knots, and the method I used to tie the cord ends to the top of each outer spring. The seat was completed by star lashing with diagonal cords from corner to corner. This braces the springs into a unit and also helps to support the spring hessian in the gaps between each spring. Knots are an important part of the spring lashing operation: if a seat is to retain its shape and give good service, the lashing needs to be tight and well-secured to the frame. Note the two tacks used at the end of each row of cord, and fixed to the main rails below the softwood boxing.

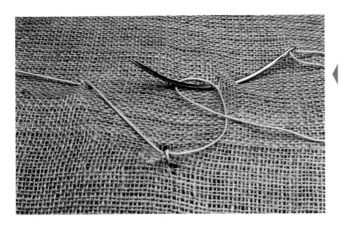

The sprung and lashed seat was then covered with 10 or 12oz hessian, pulled hand-tight and fixed with ½in (13mm) fine tacks.

Spring ties were then put in to stabilize the hessian and provide a secondary form of lashing. As you can see, the tying pattern is similar to that used under the seat. Stuffing ties were then put in around the edge of the seat and across the middle, in three rows. The seat was now ready for a first stuffing.

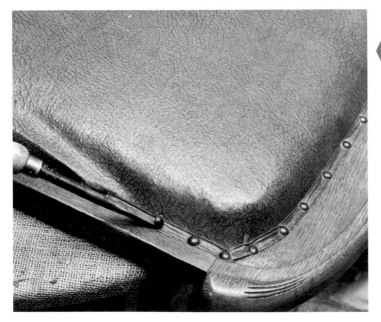

With care and gentle persuasion, the inside back upholstery was lifted and removed, beginning with the brass nails and banding. A ripping chisel was then tapped-and-levered along the length of the rails so that damage to the oak rebate would be avoided. Always have a pair of pliers or snips to hand during operations such as this, to lift out those nail shanks left in the wood when the brass heads fly off!

111

After the cover had been removed, the original stitched edge became clearly visible, having a top stuffing of washed flock. Along the rebate edge there was clear evidence of a previous cover, in the form of pieces of a deep green pile fabric still tacked below the leathercloth.

With the top stuffing removed, the whole of the original inside back covering was revealed, and proved to be a well-preserved sample of heavy wool plush, quite typical of the period. I could now safely assume that the leathercloth cover was a re-covering job performed at some point during the 1930s or '40s.

The back webbing in close-up, with enough grass seed to sow a new lawn!

◀ Samples of the original upholstery materials from the Arts and Crafts chair, photographed and kept for future reference. Photographic records of original upholstery materials along with the materials themselves are evidence of a piece of furniture's authenticity, and in a museum they would be displayed alongside the piece itself. Such records allow the upholsterer to take an informed, traditional approach when restoring period furniture.

▲
The new inside back was completed with black and white English webbing, 10oz hessian and curled hair, first stuffing in scrim. One row of blind stitching and one row of top stitching were made to hold the edges in shape. The second stuffing of curled hair and cotton felt was then pulled down in calico.

▲
An extra second stuffing was then added to the base of the back to provide lumbar support. I used small ⅜in (10mm) tacks to fix the calico.

113

I chose three different fillings for the seat upholstery. They were not dissimilar to the original mixture of fillings, but would be more resilient to wear. A good dense layer of curled fibre was followed by a finer layer of curled hair, and this was then topped with one layer of 2½oz cotton felt. The layers were then all temporarily tacked down in calico and allowed to settle overnight.

With this type of upholstery, where all the fillings are layered together, the calico covering needs to be very tight. The shape and profile of the seat are crafted at this point, and will depend on good, even tensioning. Cutting and fitting the calico began at the two back corners, allowing the calico to be set and temporarily tacked along the top of the back seat rail. The calico was then stretched forward and fixed to the front of the seat. With the calico tight, cuts could safely be made for the arm uprights. Two parallel cuts, gradually widening to the width of the arm stump, made a tongue which was then pushed down through the seat using a regulator, and then tacked off near the webbing.

The front corners were then
formed, snipped and pleated
in a single pleat, to produce a
reasonably sharp, square
corner. When the whole seat
was set and was tight, I made
a final check for any
unevenness and a good line.
The temporary tacks were
then made permanent, and the
calico trimmed very closely
along the rebate.

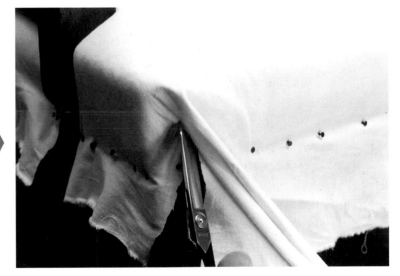

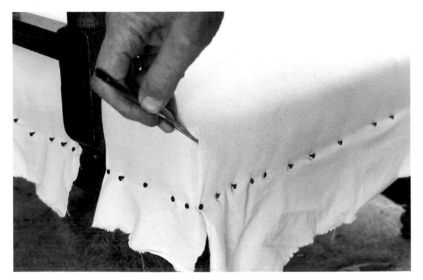

The arm pads were then stripped of their covers, and revealed more softwood boxing and a dug roll. The old washed flock was removed and replaced with a small amount of curled hair, and then overlaid with new cotton felt. The two arm pads were completed by pulling down in calico, which was well-stretched along the length of the

pads. Always remember that in upholstery covering, a long pull is always more effective than a short pull, because it gives a good line and a smooth surface to the material prior to tacking along each side.

The chair was finished in calico, with two pleats at the front and back of each arm pad. All the edges were carefully trimmed to ensure no loose or flapping edges. The whole chair was then remeasured accurately, and a cutting plan sketched out for the new cover. In this case, this helped to ensure that the bold pattern was centred on the main parts of the chair.

Final covering began with the inside back, using 10mm (⅜in) fine tacks, and some black gimp pins. The cover was centred and set in place, and then stretched from bottom to top. The two top corners, where fullness occurs, were gathered and tacked rather than pleated.

A knife and a sharp pair of scissors were used to ensure the trimming along the rebates was as accurate as possible.

The seat cover was then laid in place and centred. Cutting then began around the back legs, so that the rear edge could be pushed through the tuckaway between the seat and back, and set onto the back seat rail.

The long tongue
was then cut at the
arm stumps, once
the front seat edge
had been tacked.

The seat front corners
were then pulled down
and cut. A large square
of the fabric can be
removed before the
corner is pleated and
tacked into place.

The arm pad covers were set on with two tacks at each end, and a good pull along the length of each arm.

Gaps below each arm support were filled in using the technique of 'back tacking' a small square of fabric, using a small cardboard strip. This technique is commonly used to fill in such gaps, and where the area concerned is large, it is important to lay the fabric on its side, so that it is matched to the main seat cover.

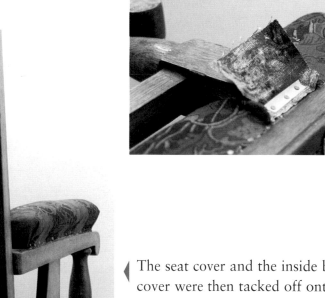

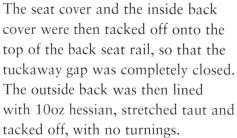

The seat cover and the inside back cover were then tacked off onto the top of the back seat rail, so that the tuckaway gap was completely closed. The outside back was then lined with 10oz hessian, stretched taut and tacked off, with no turnings.

A layer of skin wadding was trimmed and fitted over the hessian ready for the outside back cover to be tacked in place along the rebates.

Once covering was complete, the chair was stood down off the bench and given a thorough check to see that the line of the upholstery was good. At this point, you may find it helpful to look *down* on a piece, to give a different perspective. You will find that any uneven areas will show up quite clearly. Adjustments can still be made, and trimmed edges checked for cleanness, before trimmings of gimp or braid are applied. You can see here that the upholstery of the chair has turned out satisfactorily, with a good sharp line to the seat, with tight corners and a smooth crown.

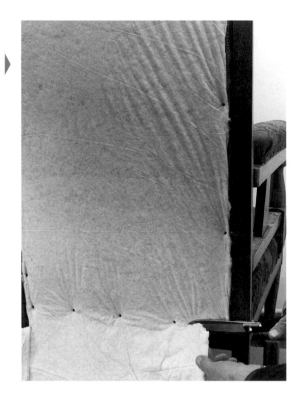

A deep-green scroll gimp was then applied using a hot-melt glue gun to give a strong, permanent bond. Each length of gimp was first back-tacked with gimp pins, and then finished by trimming and turning with a spot of glue, before gimp-pinning in place. A cold contact glue, fed from a tube, could also be used.

Finally, the chair was turned over and a dust cover of black cotton lining fitted under the seat.

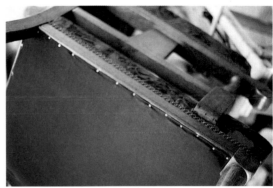

At each leg corner, the lining was turned back and cut down the middle before trimming off the excess, and then turning and tacking.

The finished chair.

121

9 Late Victorian chaise longue c.1885

The chaise longue ('long chair') has a long and varied history, and similar lounging seats can be traced back as far as the Roman Empire. The design became very popular in the UK during the Victorian era, in part because it was at this time that it became socially acceptable for men and women to recline, or 'lounge' in public. During this period the chaise longue was produced in many different forms: single- and double-ended; left and right handed; ottoman styles; and even some with drop-arm mechanisms.

The chaise longue featured in this project was made towards the end of the nineteenth century and represents a very definite statement of Victorian design and proportion. The scroll end has a generous reclining slope, and the long, high backrest provides welcoming and draft-free support. The long seat and strong, turned legs with robust brass and china castors make it suitable for any size or weight of person. All this is in strong contrast to chaise longues made during the following Edwardian period, in the early part of the twentieth century, which were far more lightweight and visually delicate.

The legs, mouldings and show wood of this piece are made from mahogany, while the frame is constructed almost entirely from softwood, with a small amount of beech used for the end uprights. Very little structural restoration was required, but, as is quite common with large pieces of seating, the castors needed some repair and replacement, and the inner edges of the long backrest frame required reinforcement due to damage caused by upholstery tacking.

Removal of the existing upholstery revealed that at some point early in its life most of the original upholstery had been removed and replaced, but the job had been badly done using cheap materials.

COVERING USED
4m (13ft) of 142cm (56in) wide damask weave.

The chaise longue came to me covered in a thick, well-worn wool pile moquette. You can see one seat spring poking through a hole in the torn covering. I removed the dust cover under the seat and the outside back cover, loosening the screws in the frame and detaching the long backrest from the seat.

The stripping of the upholstery from the seat and the scroll showed how crudely the upholstery had been constructed. Woodwool (waste wood processed into long, fine strips resembling wool, which went out of fashion shortly before the Second World War) and rag flock were the main fillings, and the seat had been boxed up using lengths of softwood nailed along all the edges. The shape and proportions of the scroll-end upholstery were very flat, and lacked the graceful line that the original makers would have intended.

Once the boxed edging was removed, small pieces of the original webbings became visible on top of the rails. This clearly indicated that the original seat had not been sprung, and instead would have had a long, mattress-style cushion on it.

The inside of the backrest was still covered in its original haircloth cover. This type of coarse, hard-wearing fabric was widely used throughout the Victorian period. This gives a possible clue as to why the piece was reupholstered and given a more fashionable and comfortable cover.

The frame after stripping and cleaning, with the small amount of restoration work complete.

Long seats of this type depend on a strong base with plenty of firmly stretched webbing. I used 12lb jute webbing, fixed with 16mm (⅝in) tacks on the seat and 13mm (½in) fine on the scroll end. Note that the bottom web on the scroll is folded lengthways to give a double thickness so as to provide support at the tuckaway point, where all the materials will meet and be pushed through to be fixed to the end seat rail.

When rewebbing an old piece of furniture, especially one with a softwood frame such as this, always avoid the original webbing positions and use fresh timber to fix the new webs. Using the old positions, even if the tack holes have been filled, will inevitably lead to a weaker webbing structure.

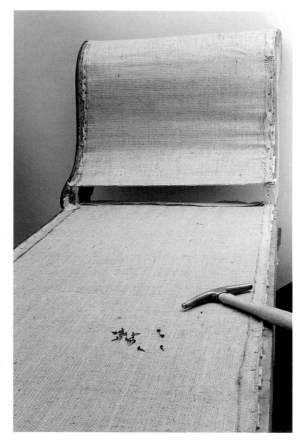

A 12oz hessian was used to cover the webbing on the seat, and a 10oz hessian on the scroll end. Both were well stretched and secured with 13mm (½in) fine tacks.

The bottom edge of the end hessian was then turned in and lock stitched to the folded webbing edge to stabilize the hessian and keep it taut when the fillings were tied in.

Curled coconut fibre was used for the first stuffing, tied in from top to bottom of the scroll end. The shape and density of the filling are very important: the bottom half is, as you can see, concave, and this will receive the bolster cushion, and is hence far more thinly filled than the top. This will produce a shallow edge which will increase in height and thickness towards the top. You can see that the filling flows over the bottom edge and fills the gap at seat level.

A piece of scrim was cut slightly over-size and temporarily tacked over the fibre. It was then bridled tightly into the lower concave area and the upper part lightly bridled with single ties over the well-filled scroll.

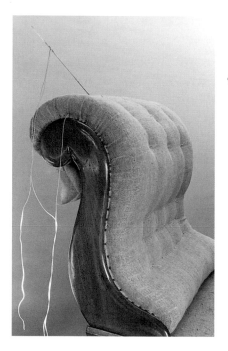

As the scrim was trimmed and tacked down, the true shape began to emerge. Some pleating and gathering was needed around the top of the scroll. The scrim was blind stitched from the top left corner down to the base, keeping as close to the tack line as possible.

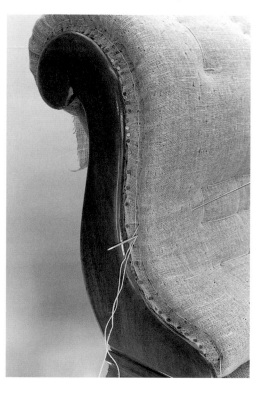

A second row of blind stitches was then worked just above the first row, stopping at the point shown by the needle.

The blind stitching was continued along the base using a 6in (152mm) curved needle, taking the needle out of the scrim and returning it into the same hole at an angle. This method is always used to create a blind stitch using a curved needle when space is restricted and a straight needle cannot be used. This blind stitch lifts the stuffing and lightly firms the edge against which the long seat cushion will rest.

The scroll edge was then given definition with one row of top stitches, running the whole way down to seat level. Foundation work such as the preceding five stages is an important part of traditional upholstery, and demonstrates the need to visualize how the finished piece will look when you are building an edge. Where possible, always set the scrim tacking line well back from the show-wood edge, so as to allow enough space for subsequent fillings and coverings, plus, if applicable, a braid or gimp finish.

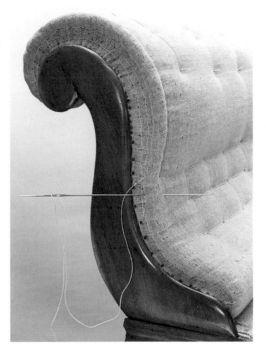

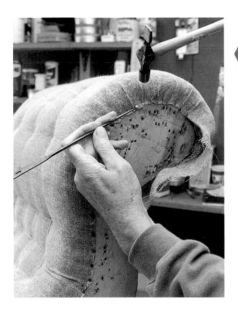

The backrest side of the scroll end was then permanently pleated, tacked in, and given one row of blind stitching to support and firm up the edge. I used the smallest fine tacks here, to minimize damage to the frame edges.

A second stuffing, this time of curled hair was then tied in very thinly at the base, becoming progressively thicker towards the top of the scroll, being careful to retain the shape.

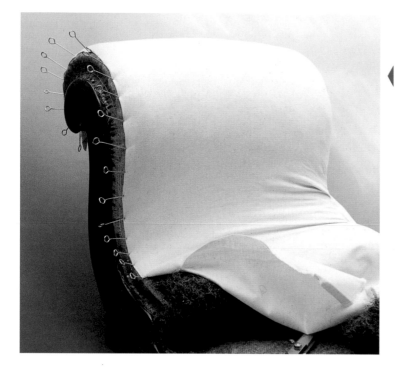

A covering of calico was then well stretched from left to right over the back and fixed in place with temporary tacks and skewers.

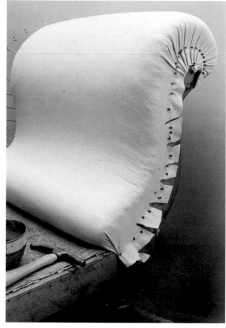

The rear end facing was then pulled down and set with temporary tacks. To ease the tension in the curve, the calico was split several times as tacking proceeded. At the top of the scroll a good firm pull was required, and a series of pleats worked in for a neat finish.

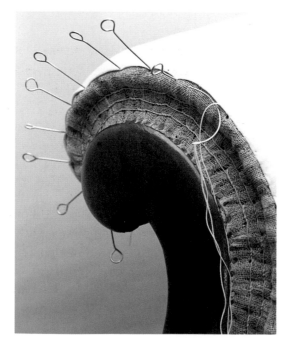

The end was completed in calico by turning-in on the face edge and slip stitching. Remember to make sure tightness is maintained by the stitching before the skewers are removed.

Seats are referred to as platforms when they support a cushion, and the upholstery of the chaise longue platform began with the cover back tacked to the long front edge. The other two, shorter edges had a narrow, folded strip of cover set closely along the show-wood edges and fixed with a cardboard strip. The folded edges were left just visible and protruding by between 2–3mm (¹⁄₁₆–¹⁄₈in), to provide a fixing point on to which the platform can be slip stitched and finished.

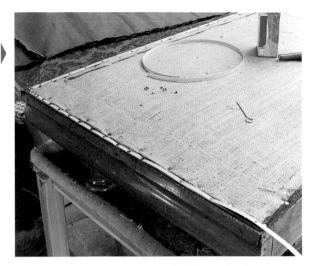

Here you can see the platform filling in place (one layer of 2½oz cotton felt cut exactly to the seat size), and the cover in place, which is made up from three pieces of the show-fabric, machined round a strong platform cloth.

The platform was then slip stitched and the back edge tacked in place with fine tacks. Because the platform would need to flex when in use, the fabric must not be over-stretched or set too tightly.

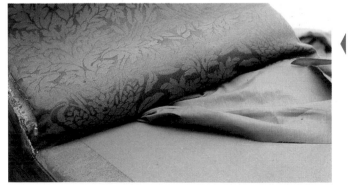

The platform covering was then completed by cutting to a point just inside the end uprights, so that it could be pushed through the tuckaway and then tacked and finished on top of the end seat rail.

Three rows of tufting stitches were then put into the lower curve of the scroll end to maintain shape before final covering. These were simply individual threads of white stitching twine, catching the calico, with a slip knot back to the webbings.

The cover was tried on for fit and then a 'fly piece' made from some left over platform cloth was sewn along the bottom edge in order to save about 8in (203mm) of fabric. In a similar situation you may well decide the use of a fly piece is unnecessary, and cut the whole thing from covering fabric. However, the use of fly pieces like this is common in commercial situations where substantial savings can be made to materials being used in large quantities. Two thicknesses of skin wadding were laid over the calico, trimmed to the edge line and tucked well in under the base. The wadding, cover and fly piece can all be seen here.

Like the calico, the cover was tacked and pleated at the back having been well stretched over the scroll and tightly pulled across the lower curved area.

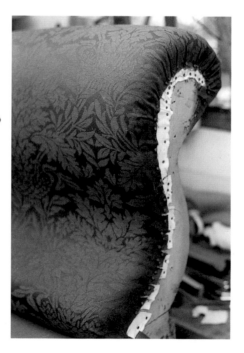

The front-facing edge on the show-wood side (the front) was turned and slip stitched using the same method as for the calico. A long narrow strip was then cut to form the pleated facing, which was pinned and pleated at intervals down the length of the scroll curve, using plenty of small pins. Before it was tacked down, a length of cotton felt was inserted behind the facing to fill it out.

The next stage was to restore the backrest, beginning with the webbing in a pattern of six vertical webs interlaced with two horizontal ones.

The webbing was then covered with 10oz hessian and the first stuffing tied in to a thickness of about 2in (51mm). The filling was thinned off and stopped above the bottom rail and inside the scroll end rail to ensure that the backrest would fit back onto the main frame snugly.

Next, the linen scrim was trimmed
roughly to shape and temporarily
tacked reasonably tight. Two rows
of bridle ties were stitched in and
all the edges turned in and tacked.

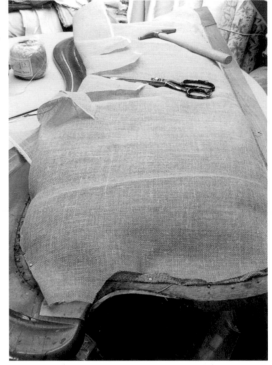

The top outer edge was then blind stitched using the 'mattress stitch' technique, in
which a large, curved needle is used in a zig-zag movement along the edge. You can see
the small stitches this produces just above the tacks. As each stitch is made, the twine
should be pulled hard to draw the filling into the edge. This simple stitch produces a
firm rounded edge in the same way as a conventional blind stitch, but does not produce
quite such a sharp, hard line, making it ideal for the backs of chairs and settees. It
originates from mid-eighteenth century cushion- and mattress-making techniques.

The back was then
checked for fit against
the seat and end
before the second
stuffing and the cover
were applied. I used a
soft pencil to mark a
line along the inside of
the scroll and the seat
platform, so that I
knew where to stop
the second stuffing.

Two layers of cotton felt were laid over the scrim and trimmed to the edge line. No calico lining was used because it was not strictly necessary here, and this simplified the back upholstery. The cover was then set on with temporary tacks.

At this point, the patterned upholstery cover for the backrest was set on and checked to ensure that it would line up with and match the seat cushion covering. The cushion top cover was measured and cut, and then laid out on the platform, and the backrest fabric adjusted to ensure a pattern-match.

Fine ¼in (6mm) tacks were used to fix the backrest cover in place. The fabric was well stretched horizontally, before being tacked into the show-wood rebate. The pattern was then checked for alignment before the tacks were made permanent. A pair of sharply pointed utility scissors were then used to trim along the show-wood rebates.

The next stage was to make up the cushions: a single long seat cushion and a bolster. These were made up in cambric and filled with a mixture of 60% feathers and 40% down. 16lb (7.25kg) of this mixture were needed for the seat, and 3lb (1.4kg) for the bolster. The main seat was divided into four parts with three dividing strips of cambric sewn to the top and bottom panels. These strips were cut to be 2in (51mm) deeper than the border depth to allow the centre of the cushion to 'crown' once it was filled. The cushion cases were made up to be 1in (25mm) larger all round than the finished cover size to allow the cushion covers to be well filled. This, in addition to the four separate sections, made sure that filling was plentiful and that once filled, the feathers and down would not be able to 'move' and alter the shape of the cushion as a result of it being sat on.

The division lines were drawn onto the top and bottom panels, ready for sewing.

The bolster ends were then drawn to fit the curve of the upholstered scroll end. As the required diameter in this case was 180mm (7⅛in), an average-size tea plate proved an ideal template. This diameter gave a sewing allowance of 10mm (⅜in), so that the bolster would have a finished diameter of approximately 160mm (6¼in).

The case was then closed with a closing seam, leaving one long side open for filling.

The seat cushion was then filled and closed.

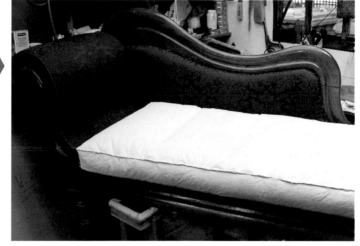

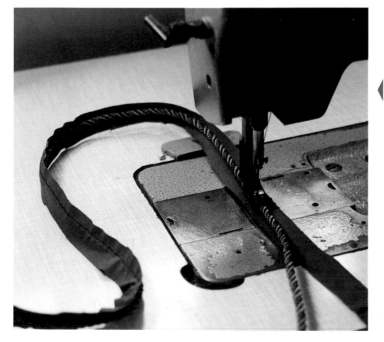

Upholstery cord for the cushion covers was then flanged by machining to a cotton strip using a ¼in (6mm) piping foot on the sewing machine. The needle catches the edge of the cord down onto the strip, which was then folded to form the flanged cord.

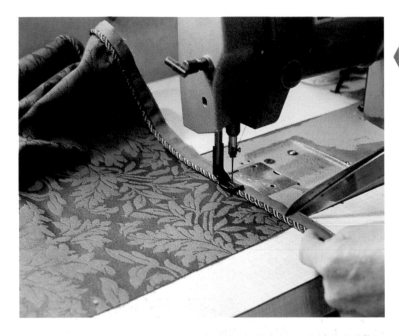

All the parts for the seat cushion cover were measured from the chaise longue, for a good, accurate fit, with a sewing allowance of ⅜in (10mm). Paper templates are sometimes helpful here, to which a sewing allowance would be added when cutting the material. The flanged cord was then sewn around the top and bottom panels. The flange was snipped at the corners to allow it to open and flex, and hence follow their contour accurately.

The long cushion was then assembled and the 4in (102mm) borders cut to length and sewn around the corded panels, joining at each corner.

The bolster cover was then cut and prepared. The main panel was cut ½in (13mm) shorter than the width of the seat cushion to allow for the extra depth of stuffing in the upper part of the backrest. Sewing began with the cord sewn around the two circular ends.

The completed bolster was then filled and adjusted for shape before being closed with a neat slip stitch.

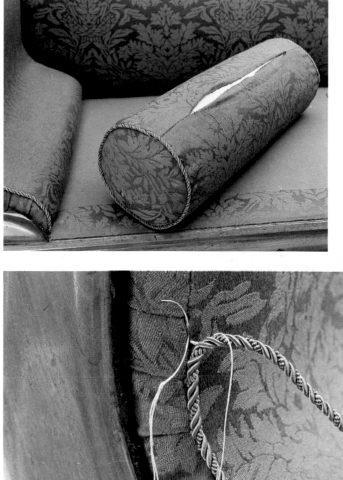

The scroll-end facing was then trimmed by slip stitching the cording onto the edge join using a small cording needle. A smooth, even line as the cord is twisted and stitched is essential here, and in the photograph you can see the stitch interval and the thread caught into the underside of the cord. The thread was pulled tight after every three or four stitches to maintain a close fit and a good line.

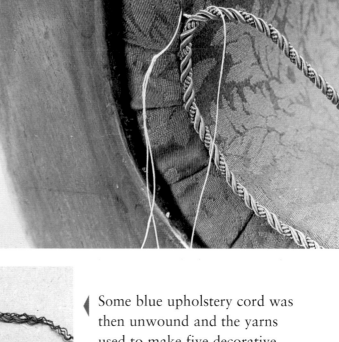

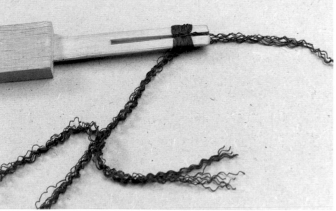

Some blue upholstery cord was then unwound and the yarns used to make five decorative tufts. Each tuft required six winds around the tufting stick, and was then cross-wound twice to draw the centre into a floret. When slid off the stick, the cross-winds were tightened and knotted on the back of the tuft.

139

A length of fine twine was then needled into the back of each tuft and pulled into the upholstery. A double slip knot and a fabric toggle were used to hold the tufts tightly to the webbing base. While adding a decorative embellishment, the tufts also served to stabilize the cover where the bolster would rest.

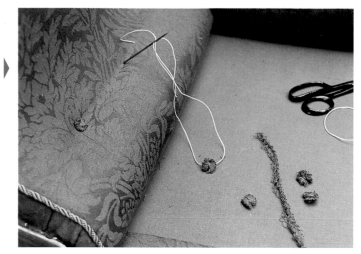

The outside back frame was then lined and prepared with a hessian support and a layer of skin wadding. The cover was then applied and tacked along the show-wood line.

The chaise longue was then turned over on the bench and the outside end webbed across the frame and then lined with wadding to support the final cover. This was then back tacked at the top and turned in before being slip stitched at the back corners. The underside of the seat was then lined with a black cotton dust cover.

The chaise longue was then turned the right way up again and upholstery gimp glued around all the show-wood edges. In total this project used up 10.5m of upholstery cord, and 8m of scroll gimp!

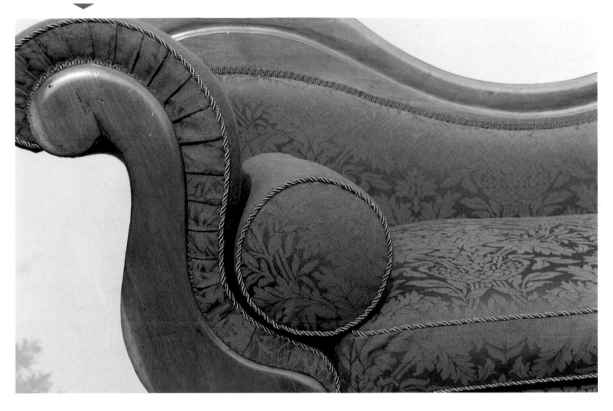

The finished piece.

History of furniture

Principal British styles

	Approximate dates	Monarchs
Elizabethan	1588–1603	Elizabeth I
Jacobean	1603–1625	James I
Carolean	1625–1649	Charles I
Cromwellian	1649–1660	Commonwealth
Restoration	1660–1689	Charles II (d.1685)
		James II (d.1689)
William and Mary	1689–1702	William and Mary (Mary d.1694)
Queen Anne	1702–1714	Anne
Early Georgian	1714–1727	George I
Georgian	1727–1760	George II
Late Georgian	1760–1810	George III (d.1820)
Regency	1810–1830	George IV
William IV	1830–1837	William IV
Victorian	1837–1901	Victoria
Edwardian	1901–1910	Edward VII

Principal French styles

	Approximate dates		Approximate dates
Louis XIV	1660–1700	*Directoire*	1790–1800
Régence	1700–1715	*Consulat* and Empire	1800–1815
Louis XV	1715–1765	Restoration	1815–1830
Transitional	1765–1775	Louis Phillipe	1830–1848
Louis XVI	1775–1790	Second Empire	1848–1870

Principal European styles and influences

Renaissance Revival of ancient Greek and Roman styles in fourteenth- and fifteenth-century Italy. Widespread by the sixteenth century.

Baroque Massive and exuberant forms of classical inspiration during the seventeenth and early eighteenth centuries.

Rococo Light, asymmetrical, scrolling designs developed in France in the early eighteenth century.

Chinoiserie Often fanciful interest in China from the late seventeenth century to the early nineteenth century.

Gothic revival Romantic interpretations of medieval (pre-Renaissance) styles in late eighteenth- and early nineteenth-century Britain.

Neoclassicism Renewed interest in the styles of classical antiquity from the mid-eighteenth to the early nineteenth centuries.

Regency Opulent melding of classical and romantic styles in early nineteenth-century Britain.

Historical revivals Several styles were favoured in nineteenth-century Britain (with equivalents elsewhere): Classical, Gothic, Elizabethan and Louis XIV.

Arts and Crafts Emphasis on hand skills and traditional designs in late nineteenth-century Britain.

Art Nouveau Organic flowing forms and geometrical abstraction are two variations on this turn-of-the-century style.

Art Deco Fine materials and streamlined forms characterize this early twentieth-century style originated in France.

Useful addresses

Furniture

**British Antique Dealers
Association** (BADA)
20 Rutland Gate, Knightsbridge,
London, SW7 1BD

**British Antique Furniture
Restorers Association** (BAFRA)
37 Upper Addison Gardens,
Holland Park, London, W14 8AJ

**London and Provincial Antique Dealers
Association** (LAPADA)
535 Kings Road,
London, SW10 0SZ

**British Furniture
Manufacturers** (BFM)
30 Harcourt Street,
London, W1H 2AA

The Furniture History Society
78 Redcliffe Square,
London, SW10 9BN

The Regional Furniture Society
The Trout House, Warrens Cross,
Lechlade, Gloucester, GL7 3DR

**The Worshipful Company
of Furniture Makers**
Painters Hall, 9 Little Trinity Lane,
London, EC4V 2AD

**The International Antique and
Collectors Fairs** (IACF),
Contactable on 01636 702326, they
organize a large number of fairs
countrywide throughout the year, particularly large outdoor markets during the
summer months. A huge range of
furniture can be seen and purchased at
such events.

Another source of information and
supply is the *The Antique Trade Gazette*,
which can be ordered from any good
newsagent.

Upholstery

**Association of Master Upholsterers and
Soft Furnishers** (AMU)
Francis Vaughan House,
102 Commercial Street,
Newport, Gwent, NP9 1LU

Guild of Traditional Upholsterers
141 Castle Street, Salisbury,
Wiltshire, SP1 2TP
(Membership Secretary
c/o 1 Salisbury Street,
Marnhul, Sturminster Newton,
Dorset, DT10 1HP)

**The Worshipful Company
of Upholders**
102 Commercial Street,
Newport, Gwent, NP9 1LU

Conservation and training

**The Conservation Unit,
Museums and Galleries Commission**
16 Queen Anne Gate,
London, SW1 9AA

Rural Development Commision
141 Castle Street, Salisbury,
Wiltshire, SP1 2TP

Calculation tables

Length centimetres	cm or inches	inches
2.54	1	0.39
5.08	2	0.79
7.62	3	1.18
10.16	4	1.58
12.70	5	1.97
15.24	6	2.36
17.78	7	2.76
20.32	8	3.15
22.86	9	3.54
25.40	10	3.94

Weight kilograms	kg or pounds	pounds
0.45	1	2.21
0.91	2	4.41
1.36	3	6.61
1.81	4	8.82
2.27	5	11.02
2.72	6	13.23
3.18	7	15.43
3.63	8	17.64
4.08	9	19.84
4.45	10	22.05

To convert	Multiply by
Length	
Inches to centimetres	2.54
Centimetres to inches	0.3937
Feet to metres	0.3048
Metres to feet	3.2808
Yards to metres	0.9144
Metres to yards	1.0936
Area	
Sq inches to sq centimetres	6.4516
Sq centimetres to sq inches	0.155
Sq feet to sq metres	0.0929
Sq metres to sq feet	10.7639
Sq yards to sq metres	0.8361
Sq metres to sq yards	1.1959

To convert	Multiply by
Volume	
Cu inches to cu centimetres	16.387
Cu centimetres to cu inches	0.06102
Cu feet to cu metres	0.02831
Cu metres to cu feet	35.3147
Cu yards to cu metres	0.76455
Cu metres to cu yards	1.30795
Weight	
Ounces to grams	28.3495
Grams to ounches	0.03527
Pounds to grams	453.59
Grams to pounds	0.002204
Pounds to kilograms	0.45359
Kilograms to pounds	2.2046

Choosing the right needle and thread for upholstery sewing

	Lightweight upholstery	Medium upholstery	Heavy upholstery
Needle size	18 Singer 110 metric	19 Singer 120 metric	21 Singer 130 metric
Thread size	75	50/36	36

Stitch density for upholstery sewing

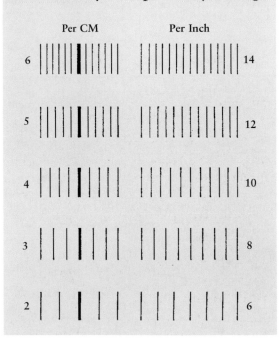

Index

About the author

The beech tree produces one of the best known hardwoods used in the construction of upholstered chair frames, and this tree grows in profusion in the Chiltern Hills around High Wycombe, where David James was born. David has spent most of his working life in the furniture industry, including the areas of further and higher education, and consultancy. He is presently a member of the lecturing team at Buckinghamshire College (High Wycombe), and teaches the BA (Hons) Furniture Restoration course.

He is an honorary member of the City and Guilds of London Institute, and has been awarded their Licentiateship.

He is also an active member of the Guild of Traditional Upholsterers, and a member of the Association of Master Upholsterers.

In recent years David has turned his talents to writing and illustrating, and has written three previous books, all published by GMC Publications: *Upholstery: A Complete Course* (1990), *Upholstery Techniques and Projects* (1994) and *The Upholsterer's Pocket Reference Book* (1995). He has also made two videos: *The Traditional Upholstery Workshop, Part 1: Drop-in and Pinstuffed Seats*, and *The Traditional Upholstery Workshop, Part 2: Stuffover Upholstery* (both 1994).

150

TITLES AVAILABLE FROM
GMC PUBLICATIONS

BOOKS

WOODTURNING

Adventures in Woodturning	*David Springett*	Practical Tips for Turners & Carvers	*GMC Publications*
Bert Marsh: Woodturner	*Bert Marsh*	Practical Tips for Woodturners	*GMC Publications*
Bill Jones' Notes from the Turning Shop	*Bill Jones*	Spindle Turning	*GMC Publications*
Bill Jones' Further Notes from the Turning Shop	*Bill Jones*	Turning Miniatures in Wood	*John Sainsbury*
Carving on Turning	*Chris Pye*	Turning Wooden Toys	*Terry Lawrence*
Colouring Techniques for Woodturners	*Jan Sanders*	Understanding Woodturning	*Ann & Bob Phillips*
Decorative Techniques for Woodturners	*Hilary Bowen*	Useful Woodturning Projects	*GMC Publications*
Faceplate Turning: Features, Projects, Practice	*GMC Publications*	Woodturning: A Foundation Course	*Keith Rowley*
Green Woodwork	*Mike Abbott*	Woodturning Jewellery	*Hilary Bowen*
Illustrated Woodturning Techniques	*John Hunnex*	Woodturning Masterclass	*Tony Boase*
Keith Rowley's Woodturning Projects	*Keith Rowley*	Woodturning: A Source Book of Shapes	*John Hunnex*
Make Money from Woodturning	*Ann & Bob Phillips*	Woodturning Techniques	*GMC Publications*
Multi-Centre Woodturning	*Ray Hopper*	Woodturning Wizardry	*David Springett*
Pleasure & Profit from Woodturning	*Reg Sherwin*		

WOODCARVING

The Art of the Woodcarver	*GMC Publications*	Understanding Woodcarving	*GMC Publications*
Carving Birds & Beasts	*GMC Publications*	Wildfowl Carving Volume 1	*Jim Pearce*
Carving Realistic Birds	*David Tippey*	Wildfowl Carving Volume 2	*Jim Pearce*
Carving on Turning	*Chris Pye*	The Woodcarvers	*GMC Publications*
Decorative Woodcarving	*Jeremy Williams*	Woodcarving: A Complete Course	*Ron Butterfield*
Essential Woodcarving Techniques	*Dick Onians*	Woodcarving for Beginners: Projects, Techniques & Tools	
Lettercarving in Wood	*Chris Pye*		*GMC Publications*
Practical Tips for Turners & Carvers	*GMC Publications*	Woodcarving Tools, Materials & Equipment	*Chris Pye*

PLANS, PROJECTS, TOOLS & THE WORKSHOP

The Incredible Router	*Jeremy Broun*	Sharpening Pocket Reference Book	*Jim Kingshott*
Making & Modifying Woodworking Tools	*Jim Kingshott*	The Workshop	*Jim Kingshott*
Sharpening: The Complete Guide	*Jim Kingshott*		

TOYS & MINIATURES

Designing & Making Wooden Toys	*Terry Kelly*	Making Wooden Toys & Games	*Jeff & Jennie Loader*
Fun to Make Wooden Toys & Games	*Jeff & Jennie Loader*	Miniature Needlepoint Carpets	*Janet Granger*
Making Board, Peg & Dice Games	*Jeff & Jennie Loader*	Turning Miniatures in Wood	*John Sainsbury*
Making Little Boxes from Wood	*John Bennett*	Turning Wooden Toys	*Terry Lawrence*

CREATIVE CRAFTS

Celtic Knotwork Designs	*Sheila Sturrock*	Embroidery Tips & Hints	*Harold Hayes*
Collage from Seeds, Leaves and Flowers	*Joan Carver*	Making Knitwear Fit	*Pat Ashforth & Steve Plummer*
The Complete Pyrography	*Stephen Poole*	Miniature Needlepoint Carpets	*Janet Granger*
Creating Knitwear Designs	*Pat Ashforth & Steve Plummer*	Tatting Collage	*Lindsay Rogers*
Cross Stitch on Colour	*Sheena Rogers*		

UPHOLSTERY AND FURNITURE

Care & Repair	GMC Publications	Making Shaker Furniture	Barry Jackson
Complete Woodfinishing	Ian Hosker	Pine Furniture Projects	Dave Mackenzie
Furniture Projects	Rod Wales	Seat Weaving (Practical Crafts)	Ricky Holdstock
Furniture Restoration (Practical Crafts)	Kevin Jan Bonner	Upholsterer's Pocket Reference Book	David James
Furniture Restoration & Repair for Beginners	Kevin Jan Bonner	Upholstery: A Complete Course	David James
Green Woodwork	Mike Abbott	Upholstery: Techniques & Projects	David James
Making Fine Furniture	Tom Darby	Woodfinishing Handbook (Practical Crafts)	Ian Hosker

DOLLS' HOUSES & DOLLS' HOUSE FURNITURE

Architecture for Dolls' Houses	Joyce Percival	Making Period Dolls' House Accessories	Andrea Barham
A Beginners' Guide to the Dolls' House Hobby	Jean Nisbett	Making Period Dolls' House Furniture	Derek & Sheila Rowbottom
The Complete Dolls' House Book	Jean Nisbett	Making Victorian Dolls' House Furniture	Patricia King
Easy-to-Make Dolls' House Accessories	Andrea Barham	Miniature Needlepoint Carpets	Janet Granger
Make Your Own Dolls' House Furniture	Maurice Harper	The Secrets of the Dolls' House Makers	Jean Nisbett
Making Dolls' House Furniture	Patricia King		

OTHER BOOKS

Guide to Marketing	GMC Publications	Woodworkers' Career & Educational Source Book	GMC Publications

VIDEOS

Carving a Figure: The Female Form	Ray Gonzalez	Woodturning: A Foundation Course	Keith Rowley
The Traditional Upholstery Workshop		Elliptical Turning	David Springett
Part 1: Drop-in & Pinstuffed Seats	David James	Woodturning Wizardry	David Springett
The Traditional Upholstery Workshop		Turning Between Centres: The Basics	Dennis White
Part 2: Stuffover Upholstery	David James	Turning Bowls	Dennis White
Hollow Turning	John Jordan	Boxes, Goblets & Screw Threads	Dennis White
Bowl Turning	John Jordan	Novelties & Projects	Dennis White
Sharpening Turning & Carving Tools	Jim Kingshott	Classic Profiles	Dennis White
Sharpening the Professional Way	Jim Kingshott	Twists & Advanced Turning	Dennis White

MAGAZINES

WOODTURNING • WOODCARVING • TOYMAKING

FURNITURE & CABINETMAKING • BUSINESSMATTERS

• CREATIVE IDEAS FOR THE HOME

The above represents a full list of all titles currently published or scheduled to be published. All are available direct from the Publishers or through bookshops, newsagents and specialist retailers. To place an order, or to obtain a complete catalogue, contact:

GMC Publications, 166 High Street, Lewes, East Sussex BN7 1XU United Kingdom
Tel: 01273 488005 Fax: 01273 478606
Orders by credit card are accepted